If you are waiting for a sign, something to show you that you are exactly where you need to be, this is it.

Keep going...

The 30-Day Ultimate Closet Guide

A STEP-BY-STEP GUIDE TO GETTING
THE WARDROBE YOU'VE ALWAYS WANTED.

BRITTANY WITKIN

Copyright © 2014 The BWIT Group LLC

All rights reserved.

ISBN-10: 069228463X
ISBN-13: 978-0692284636

DEDICATION

I'd like to dedicate this book to my parents Gary and Judy. Thank you for believing in my dreams, even (especially) the really crazy ones.

I love you both beyond words.

CONTENTS:

The Ultimate Closet, Defined — Pg. 5

The Closet Toolkit — Pg. 11

Week 1: Make Space — Pg. 43

Week 2: The Outfit Blueprint — Pg. 69

Week 3: Looks Come to Life — Pg. 95

Week 4: Rinse & Repeat — Pg. 105

THE (ULTIMATE) CLOSET CONVERSATION:

"Thanks to The 30-Day Ultimate Closet Guide, I have once again embraced my inner (and now outer) fashionista! This guide is much more than a closet revamp. It is really a life organizer. With the quick tips, and easy-to-follow graphics (especially the outfit planner template) I am on my way to an organized closet and a more organized life!" -Roberta Martone Pavia, Consultant/Writer/Mother

"A weakness for clearance sales had left my closet in shambles. Getting ready for work/a night out was a major undertaking, often resulting in half of my wardrobe on the floor. I knew I needed to do something, but I didn't know where to start. After walking through Brittany's incredibly user-friendly 30-Day Ultimate Closet Guide, not only is my closet curated and organized with key pieces I love, but my morning routine is now completely stress-free and I leave the house looking and feeling my best."
-Kate Martin, Philanthropy Advisor/World Traveler

"I now know what to wear, what NOT to wear, and why it is so important to take care of myself. The 30-Day Ultimate Closet Guide has helped me clean a closet of clutter and opened the door for me to define my personal style." -Angela Wagner, Business Owner/Mother

BRITTANY WITKIN

{THE ULTIMATE CLOSET, DEFINED}

The definition of an Ultimate Closet is:

A closet filled with a high-functioning wardrobe tailored to your lifestyle so you can grab, go, and look your best without having to think about it.

After overhauling and updating the closets of over two hundred women across the country, I can tell you without hesitation, that there is a significant difference between a clean closet and an *Ultimate Closet*.

A clean closet is organized, streamlined and easy to work with. An Ultimate Closet is a clean closet, on steroids.

An Ultimate Closet is about feeling empowered to be your best self and live your best life as you walk out the door every day.

The transformation is both an external and internal one. When a client begins to realize that, not only is her closet on-point, but, she knows exactly what to do with what is in there, something magical happens.

It's like watching a switch flip on. All of a sudden the look in her eyes, her tone of voice, and the way she looks at herself in the mirror, changes. A weight is visibly lifted and she starts to see the big (or in this case, *ultimate*) picture.

What was once a full closet with nothing to wear is now a streamlined closet with plenty of updated outfit options.

I flipped my own personal style 'switch' over a decade ago after realizing that my college-student wardrobe was completely out of alignment with my new corporate role in the buying offices at Neiman Marcus. I needed an upgrade, and like so many others, I wasn't sure where to start, so I decided my tiny Dallas apartment closet would be as good of a starting point as any.

A decade in the fashion industry and hundreds of personal styling clients later, it is time to share my Ultimate Closet process with you.

I believe everyone deserves to experience what it feels like to have an Ultimate Closet, whether they have the budget to hire a personal stylist or not. My hope is that this guide will enable and empower any woman, anywhere, to create the wardrobe she has always wanted, so she can feel confident walking out the door every day.

Women all over the country (and world for that matter) are opening up the doors to their Ultimate Closets right now. Soon, you will be one of them.

Why Thirty Days?

Full disclosure: I get nothing done without a deadline.

This guide is all about keeping it simple while creating real change, and time limits are always good for that.

I have outlined all the steps on the 30-Day Calendar (part of your Closet Toolkit) so you know what to do, when to do it, and have the flexibility to make it work for your lifestyle/schedule.

Five Things You Need To Know About This Guide:

1. All worksheets and materials I reference in the steps can be found in the Closet Toolkit at the beginning of the guide (starting on page 11). You can access bonus styling tools on-line by following the links I provide.
2. The 30-Day Calendar worksheet (find it in the Week 1 Closet Toolkit, page 12) will be your best friend throughout the next thirty days. Know it, love it, sync it to your e-calendar, keep it close by, you get the picture.

3. If you want to receive the latest updates, additions, and promotions for the guide, subscribe to my mailing list here (completely optional):

   http://bit.ly/ultimateclosetguidesubscribe

4. You will notice that some of the steps have time estimates, while others do not. There is a reason for that. Spending too much time on something that is meant to be simple defeats the purpose of the process. Less thought, more action.

5. Above all, don't take it too seriously. I don't. Have fun with the next thirty days. I alternate 'fun' steps with 'get it done' steps to keep the mood light. Life is too short not to crack a smile or have a giggle fit now and then. Both are highly encouraged by the way.

Ok, time to dig into the Closet Toolkit (page 11)…

THE 30-DAY ULTIMATE CLOSET GUIDE

the closet toolkit

Welcome to the Closet Toolkit.
The next few pages are filled with exclusive styling tools I have developed to successfully transform hundreds of wardrobes across the country, and now, they are all yours!

Flip through and preview what you will be working with for the next 30 days as you go step-by-step to create your own Ultimate Closet.

You will also see links throughout this book that will take you to **(enlarged and printable)** digital versions of these tools.

Step 1 begins on page 43. Let's do this!

week 1 toolkit

Week 1, Step 1. Tool: 30-Day Closet Calendar.

WEEK 1 THE 30-DAY CALENDAR | WWW.ULTIMATECLOSETGUIDE.COM *Style shaker*

enter your starting date here
enter your starting month here

	DAY 1	DAY 2	DAY 3	DAY 4	DAY 5	DAY 6	DAY 7
WEEK 1	*Complete Baby Prep Steps *Complete Week 1, Step 1	*Start Week 1, Steps 2-4	*Finish Week 1 Steps 2-4 *Read Week 1 Step 5 the day before the Closet Overhaul	*Closet Overhaul & Re-Org Place-holder *Week 1, Steps 6-8 (3-4 hours)	*Closet Overhaul & Re-Org Place-holder *Week 1, Steps 6-8 (3-4 hours)	*Closet Overhaul & Re-Org Place-holder *Week 1, Steps 6-8 (3-4 hours)	*Finish up Closet Overhaul *Complete Week 1, Step 9
	DAY 8	**DAY 9**	**DAY 10**	**DAY 11**	**DAY 12**	**DAY 13**	**DAY 14**
WEEK 2	*Complete Week 2, Steps 1-3	*Complete Week 2, Steps 4 and 5	*Week 2, Step 6: ON-LINE Shoppers start shopping for delivery next week	*Week 2, Step 6: IN-STORE, schedule shopping ON-LINE shopping cont.	*Week 2, Step 6: Shopping placeholders, ON-LINE & IN-STORE	*Week 2, Step 6: Shopping placeholders, ON-LINE & IN-STORE	*Week 2, Step 6: Finalize shopping trip in-store, and on-line try-on/returns
	DAY 15	**DAY 16**	**DAY 17**	**DAY 18**	**DAY 19**	**DAY 20**	**DAY 21**
WEEK 3	*Complete Week 3, Step 1	*Use Outfit Planner #1 *Follow-up on shopping list where needed	*Use Outfit Planner #1 *Follow-up on shopping list where needed	*Use Outfit Planner #1 *Steps 2 and 3	*Use Outfit Planner #1 *Follow-up on shopping list where needed	*Use Outfit Planner #1 *Follow-up on shopping list where needed	*Complete Week 3, Step 4 *Follow-up on shopping list where needed
	DAY 22	**DAY 23**	**DAY 24**	**DAY 25**	**DAY 26**	**DAY 27**	**DAY 28**
WEEK 4	*Complete Week 4, Step 1	*Use Outfit Planner #2 *Follow-up on shopping list where needed	*Use Outfit Planner #2 *Follow-up on shopping list where needed	*Use Outfit Planner #2 *Complete Week 4, Steps 2 and 3	*Use Outfit Planner #2 *Follow-up on shopping list where needed	*Use Outfit Planner #2 *Follow-up on shopping list where needed	*Follow-up on shopping list where needed
	DAY 29 *Week 4, Step 4, BONUS DAY!	**DAY 30** *Week 4, Step 4, BONUS DAY!					

The BWIT Group. Copyright 2014. All rights reserved. TM pending.

THE 30-DAY ULTIMATE CLOSET GUIDE

 # week 1 toolkit

Week 1, Step 3. Tool: Closet Overhaul Contract.

WEEK 1 CLOSET CONTRACT | WWW.ULTIMATECLOSETGUIDE.COM **Style shaker**

✂ cut along this line

I, _____ [your name here], promise to stick to the timeline I have scheduled on my calendar. I will not exceed four hours for my closet overhaul/Purge & Re-Org. I know the point is to act and I promise myself that is exactly what I will do.

I, _____ [your name here], will have made space and re-organized my closet by / /2014.

I'm sending this to _____ [friend's name here] for support and to hold me accountable to my closet overhaul actions. In exchange, I will give said 'accountability bestie' something to show my appreciation whether it's a hug, glass of wine, a cupcake, proceeds from the clothing I'm about to sell on-line, a puppy, or all of the above.

_____ ♥ _____
[your signature]   [date]

_____   _____ ♥
[your friend's signature]   [date]

• DON'T FORGET! VIEW THE TOOLKIT ON-LINE •

LINKS ON PAGES 119 & 120

THE 30-DAY ULTIMATE CLOSET GUIDE

 # week 1 toolkit

Week 1, Step 4. Tool: Partner In Crime Closet Invitation.

WEEK 1 PARTNER-IN-CRIME CLOSET INVITATION | WWW.ULTIMATECLOSETGUIDE.COM   Style shaker

✂ cut along this line

join me!

I'd like to officially invite you to be my partner-in-crime for my closet overhaul!

There will be wine/sparkling water/champagne, there will be hangers, there will be a ton of laughter and possibly, a spontaneous dance party.

I couldn't think of a better friend to have by my side. Are you in?

WHEN: / /   @ :
WHERE: my closet

DON'T FORGET! VIEW THE TOOLKIT ON-LINE

LINKS ON PAGES 119 & 120

page left blank
[so you can tear out this tool]

THE 30-DAY ULTIMATE CLOSET GUIDE

 # week 1 toolkit

Week 1, Step 6. Tool: Closet Purge Cheat Sheet.

WEEK 1 CLOSET PURGE CHEAT SHEET | WWW.ULTIMATECLOSETGUIDE.COM   Style shaker

✂ cut along this line

3 questions to ask as you go through your closet:

1.
Have you worn it in the last 6 months?

2.
Does it reflect how you want to look or was it an impulse buy?

3.
Has it seen better days?

- **DON'T FORGET! VIEW THE TOOLKIT ON-LINE** -

LINKS ON PAGES 119 & 120

page left blank
[so you can tear out this tool]

THE 30-DAY ULTIMATE CLOSET GUIDE

 ## week 1 toolkit

Week 1, Step 6. Tool: Closet Zen Card.

WEEK 1 CLOSET ZEN CARD | WWW.ULTIMATECLOSETGUIDE.COM   Style shaker

✂ cut along this line

"Ohmmmmmmmmmmmmm"

CLOSET ZEN

You have to want it more than you are afraid of it.
It's just a closet.
You can do this. Come back to the steps.
breathe, put on your favorite song, & keep going.
The closet & life you've always wanted is
waiting for you...It's happening right now, if you let it.

• DON'T FORGET! VIEW THE TOOLKIT ON-LINE •

LINKS ON PAGES 119 & 120

page left blank
[so you can tear out this tool]

THE 30-DAY ULTIMATE CLOSET GUIDE

 # week 1 toolkit

Week 1, Step 7. Tool: Closet Re-Org Checklist.

WEEK 1 CLOSET RE-ORG CHECKLIST | WWW.ULTIMATECLOSETGUIDE.COM *Style shaker*

✂ cut along this line

→ **STEP 1:**

Separate out by category (hanging):

tops, bottoms (jeans, skirts, pants)

→ **STEP 2:**

Within the category, separate out by color:

tops > all red tops > all beige tops > all black...
(rinse & repeat for other categories)

→ **STEP 3:** *use for your neutral colors mainly!*

Within the category, neutral colors, separate out by cuts (silhouettes):

tops > beige tops > tanks
tops > black tops > long sleeve tees

BRITTANY WITKIN

• DON'T FORGET! VIEW THE TOOLKIT ON-LINE •

LINKS ON PAGES 119 & 120

page left blank
[so you can tear out this tool]

THE 30-DAY ULTIMATE CLOSET GUIDE

 # week 2 toolkit

Week 2, Step 1. Tool: Outfit Planner Template.

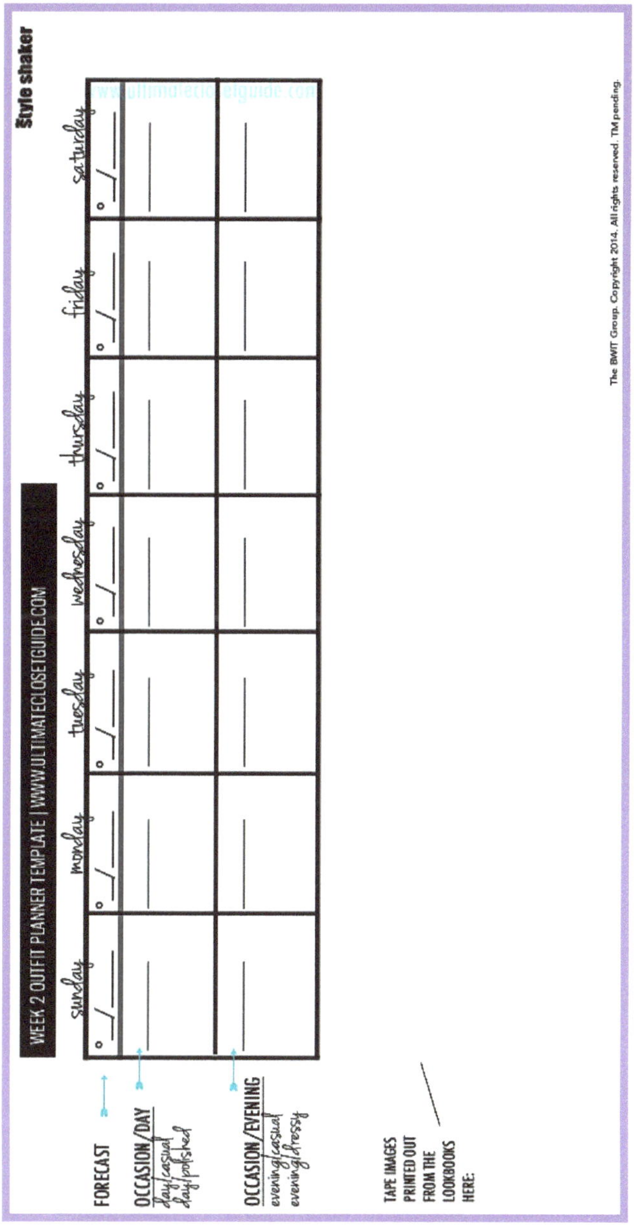

• DON'T FORGET! VIEW THE TOOLKIT ON-LINE •

LINKS ON PAGES 119 & 120

page left blank
[so you can tear out this tool]

THE 30-DAY ULTIMATE CLOSET GUIDE

 # week 2 toolkit

Week 2, Step 1. Tool: The Outfit Planner Example.

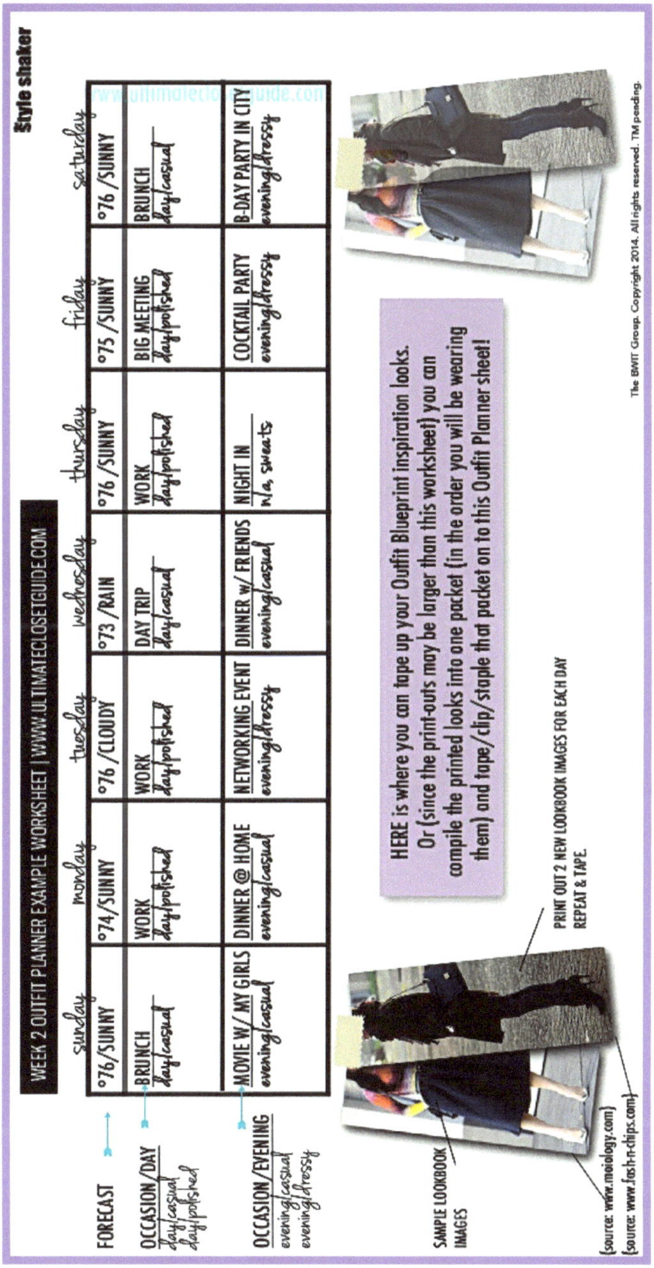

Style shaker

WEEK 2 OUTFIT PLANNER EXAMPLE WORKSHEET | WWW.ULTIMATECLOSETGUIDE.COM

	sunday	monday	tuesday	wednesday	thursday	friday	saturday
FORECAST	°76 /SUNNY	°74 /SUNNY	°76 /CLOUDY	°73 /RAIN	°76 /SUNNY	°75 /SUNNY	°76 /SUNNY
OCCASION /DAY *day/casual day/polished*	BRUNCH *day/casual*	WORK *day/polished*	WORK *day/polished*	DAY TRIP *day/casual*	WORK *day/polished*	BIG MEETING *day/polished*	BRUNCH *day/casual*
OCCASION /EVENING *evening/casual evening/dressy*	MOVIE W/ MY GIRLS *evening/casual*	DINNER @ HOME *evening/casual*	NETWORKING EVENT *evening/dressy*	DINNER w/ FRIENDS *evening/casual*	NIGHT IN *n/a, sweats*	COCKTAIL PARTY *evening/dressy*	B-DAY PARTY IN CITY *evening/dressy*

SAMPLE LOOKBOOK IMAGES

[source: www.meiology.com]
[source: www.flash-n-chips.com]

PRINT OUT 2 NEW LOOKBOOK IMAGES FOR EACH DAY. REPEAT & TAPE.

HERE is where you can tape up your Outfit Blueprint inspiration looks. Or (since the print-outs may be larger than this worksheet) you can compile the printed looks into one packet (in the order you will be wearing them) and tape/clip/staple that packet on to this Outfit Planner sheet!

The BWT Group. Copyright 2014. All rights reserved. TM pending.

• DON'T FORGET! VIEW THE TOOLKIT ON-LINE •

LINKS ON PAGES 119 & 120

page left blank
[so you can tear out this tool]

THE 30-DAY ULTIMATE CLOSET GUIDE

 # week 2 toolkit

Week 2, Step 4. Tool: Fall 80/20 Shopping List (1 of 2).

FALL 2014 (1)
WEEK 2 80/20 SHOPPING LIST | WWW.ULTIMATECLOSETGUIDE.COM — Style shaker

> [C] refers to your 'Core Closet' pieces, [T] refers to your Trend Closet Pieces, and [B] refers to your Outfit Blueprint additions!

SHOES:
- [ ] [C] classic black and nude everyday pumps
- [ ] [C] tall stacked heel boots (black and neutrals)
- [ ] [C] ankle boots (black, neutrals)
- [ ] [C] flat/riding boots (black, neutrals)
- [ ] [C] ballet and/or pointed toe flats (color/neutral)
- [ ] [T] metallic heel (evening, ankle strap, or pump)
- [ ] [T] pop color/fur accent heel (evening, ankle strap, pump)
- [ ] [T] colorful running shoes/sneakers
- [ ] [B] _____
- [ ] [B] _____
- [ ] [B] _____

HANDBAGS:
- [ ] [C] everyday shoulder bag (black)
- [ ] [C] everyday shoulder bag/tote (neutral/light)
- [ ] [C] caryall tote (color &/or neutral)
- [ ] [C] metallic everyday (large) bag
- [ ] [C] metallic &/or printed/color clutch
- [ ] [T] pop color shoulder bag &/or handheld bag
- [ ] [T] embellished or foldover clutch &/or bag
- [ ] [T] backpack (printed, fabric or neutral)
- [ ] [B] _____
- [ ] [B] _____
- [ ] [B] _____
- [ ] [B] _____

DRESSES:
- [ ] [C] L.B.D. (little black dress, sleeves optional)
- [ ] [C] long-sleeve sweater dress (black/neutrals)
- [ ] [C] sheath dress (black, neutral, with sleeve)
- [ ] [C] wrap dress (print, color or neutral/solid)
- [ ] [T] velvet (black) long and cocktail lengths
- [ ] [T] graphic, black and white prints
- [ ] [T] 60's inspired (prints, mini and trapeze shapes)
- [ ] [T] elongated dresses (tunic-esque, for over pants)
- [ ] [B] _____
- [ ] [B] _____
- [ ] [B] _____
- [ ] [B] _____

TOPS:
- [ ] [C] cardigans (neutral: black & white/grey/beige)
- [ ] [C] crewneck classic sweaters (black & neutrals)
- [ ] [C] t-shirts (neutrals, see above; v-neck or crew)
- [ ] [C] layering tanks (neutrals, see above)
- [ ] [C] white &/or chambray button-front shirt
- [ ] [C] long-sleeve tees (neutrals, see above)
- [ ] [T] elongated, embellished cozy sweaters (argyle)
- [ ] [T] oversized sweaters & knits (fairisle print-esque)
- [ ] [T] oversized, textured turtleneck knits
- [ ] [T] embellished tank (cut, metallic, peplum, sequin, etc)
- [ ] [B] _____
- [ ] [B] _____
- [ ] [B] _____
- [ ] [B] _____

JACKETS/BLAZERS:
- [ ] [C] basic black (streamlined, menswear inspired)
- [ ] [C] basic neutral (navy, grey, streamlined fit)
- [ ] [C] poncho (basic black, everyday print, or fur
- [ ] [C] leather (bomber or blazer silhouette)
- [ ] [T] sporty jackets (black, red, blue colors)
- [ ] [T] gold &/or pop color (red, etc.)
- [ ] [T] military &/or oversized denim jacket
- [ ] [T] graphic, black and white prints, leopard print
- [ ] [B] _____
- [ ] [B] _____
- [ ] [B] _____
- [ ] [B] _____

OUTERWEAR:
- [ ] [C] everyday coat (black and neutral beige/grey)
- [ ] [C] trench (black, khaki, &/or denim)
- [ ] [T] gold &/or fur-embellished (feathers too)
- [ ] [T] oversized coats & long (neutral, color, furry)
- [ ] [T] robe coats (color, neutral or print, or quilted)
- [ ] [B] _____
- [ ] [B] _____
- [ ] [B] _____
- [ ] [B] _____

The BWIT Group. Copyright 2014. All rights reserved. TM pending.

BRITTANY WITKIN

• DON'T FORGET! VIEW THE TOOLKIT ON-LINE •

LINKS ON PAGES 119 & 120

page left blank
[so you can tear out this tool]

THE 30-DAY ULTIMATE CLOSET GUIDE

week 2 toolkit

Week 2, Step 4. Tool: Fall 80/20 Shopping List (2 of 2).

FALL 2014 (2)
WEEK 2 80/20 SHOPPING LIST | WWW.ULTIMATECLOSETGUIDE.COM   *Style shaker*

[C] refers to your 'Core Closet' pieces, [T] refers to your Trend Closet Pieces, and [B] refers to your Outfit Blueprint additions!

JEANS:
- [ ] [C] everyday wear with flats (boot-cut, slight flare)
- [ ] [C] everyday wear with heels (boot-cut, slight flare)
- [ ] [C] everyday skinny
- [ ] [C] dark wash skinny
- [ ] [C] dark wash bootcut/trouser cut
- [ ] [T] embellished (embroidered, color)
- [ ] [T] high-waisted jeans
- [ ] [T] flare leg jeans
- [ ] [B] _____
- [ ] [B] _____
- [ ] [B] _____
- [ ] [B] _____

PANTS:
- [ ] [C] neutral skinny pant (black, white, olive, grey)
- [ ] [C] menswear inspired, fuller trouser pant
- [ ] [C] classic black tailored pant (straight leg)
- [ ] [C] classic grey tailored pant (straight or wider leg)
- [ ] [C] military green on any pant silhouettes
- [ ] [T] 60's inspired printed pant
- [ ] [T] Pop-color skinny leg pant
- [ ] [B] _____
- [ ] [B] _____
- [ ] [B] _____
- [ ] [B] _____

SKIRTS:
- [ ] [C] classic pencil (neutrals: black and grey)
- [ ] [C] maxi (neutrals &/or solid color)
- [ ] [C] a-line (neutral black, grey, or solid color)
- [ ] [C] mini (depending on body type)
- [ ] [C] printed &/or metallic short/pencil skirt
- [ ] [T] graphic black and white skirts
- [ ] [T] a-line denim skirts
- [ ] [T] embellished, evening option (velvet, lace)
- [ ] [B] _____
- [ ] [B] _____
- [ ] [B] _____
- [ ] [B] _____

JEWELRY:
- [ ] [C] bracelets (gold & silver, everyday classic styles)
- [ ] [C] rings (gold & silver, everyday classic styles)
- [ ] [C] earrings (gold & silver, everyday studs/hoops)
- [ ] [C] necklaces (gold & silver, chain, classic)
- [ ] [C] cuff bracelets (gold, silver, small, classic)
- [ ] [T] the single statement earring
- [ ] [T] fringed &/or leather bracelets
- [ ] [T] statement jewelry (hoops, floral necklace, leather collar/cuff, multiple rings)
- [ ] [B] _____
- [ ] [B] _____
- [ ] [B] _____

ACCESSORIES:
- [ ] [C] scarf (basic neutral or color)
- [ ] [C] sunglasses (classic, best fit for your face shape)
- [ ] [C] tights (basic black, brown, opaque)
- [ ] [T] scarves worn in place of necklaces
- [ ] [T] statement (color, prints, etc.) gloves
- [ ] [T] colorful, furry statement scarves/capes
- [ ] [T] leggings & tights (neutrals)
- [ ] [T] floral accents at the neckline (pins, scarves)
- [ ] [T] sunglasses: geometric, oversized/plastic, color, or cat-eye frames; semi/full transparent lenses (pick 1)
- [ ] [B] _____
- [ ] [B] _____
- [ ] [B] _____

The BWIT Group. Copyright 2014. All rights reserved. TM pending.

• DON'T FORGET! VIEW THE TOOLKIT ON-LINE •

LINKS ON PAGES 119 & 120

THE 30-DAY ULTIMATE CLOSET GUIDE

week 2 toolkit

Week 2, Step 4. Tool: Spring 80/20 Shopping List (1 of 2).

SPRING/SUMMER 2014 (1)
WEEK 2 80/20 SHOPPING LIST | WWW.ULTIMATECLOSETGUIDE.COM — Style shaker

[C] refers to your 'Core Closet' pieces, [T] refers to your Trend Closet Pieces, and [B] refers to your Outfit Blueprint additions!

SHOES:
- [C] heel sandal (neutral, ankle strap option)
- [C] flat sandal (neutral, cld be a soft metallic)
- [C] everyday pumps (black and neutral)
- [C] running shoes/flat walking shoes (vans-esque)
- [C] ballet and/or pointed toe flats
- [T] metallic heel (sandal, evening, pump)
- [T] pop color heel (sandal, evening, pump)
- [T] slide-on sandals, birkenstocks
- [B] _____
- [B] _____
- [B] _____
- [B] _____

HANDBAGS:
- [C] everyday shoulder bag (black)
- [C] structured 'lady' bag (color &/or neutral)
- [C] caryall tote (color &/or neutral)
- [C] everyday shoulder bag/tote (neutral/light)
- [C] clutch (metallic or neutral)
- [T] floral print/pastel clutch or top-handle bag
- [T] bucket bag (color or neutral)
- [T] backpack (printed, fabric or neutral)
- [B] _____
- [B] _____
- [B] _____
- [B] _____

DRESSES:
- [C] L.B.D. (little black dress/cocktail or sheath)
- [C] white summer dress
- [C] t-shirt dress (color, print, &/or neutral)
- [C] wrap (print, color or neutral/solid)
- [C] maxi dress (print or neutral)
- [T] jumper/romper
- [T] pastel/floral print (base cut on body type)
- [T] L.R.D. (little red dress)
- [B] _____
- [B] _____
- [B] _____
- [B] _____

TOPS:
- [C] cardigans (neutral: black & white/grey/beige)
- [C] lightweight sweaters (neutral: black & other)
- [C] t-shirts (neutrals, see above; v-neck or crew)
- [C] tanks (neutrals, see above; v-neck or crew)
- [C] white button-front shirt
- [C] long-sleeve tees (neutrals, see above)
- [T] printed/graphic knit/sweatshirt (lightweight)
- [T] print/pop color tank &/or tee, &/or crop top
- [T] contrast collar shirt
- [T] embellished tank (cut, metallic, sequin, etc)
- [B] _____
- [B] _____
- [B] _____
- [B] _____

JACKETS/BLAZERS:
- [C] basic black (streamlined)
- [C] basic white and/or grey (streamlined fit)
- [C] denim jacket (cropped or not)
- [C] lightweight military jacket
- [C] bomber/varsity jacket
- [T] cropped, boxy-shape jacket (white/color/print)
- [T] denim vest (light or dark wash)
- [T] pop color and/or pastel blazer
- [B] _____
- [B] _____
- [B] _____

OUTERWEAR:
- [C] everyday, lightweight coat (neutral)
- [C] trench (cream &/or black)
- [T] collarless coat (neutral or pastel)
- [T] graphic print/floral print coat
- [T] lightweight leather (neutral)
- [B] _____
- [B] _____
- [B] _____
- [B] _____

The BWIT Group. Copyright 2014. All rights reserved. TM pending.

DON'T FORGET! VIEW THE TOOLKIT ON-LINE

LINKS ON PAGES 119 & 120

page left blank
[so you can tear out this tool]

THE 30-DAY ULTIMATE CLOSET GUIDE

 ## week 2 toolkit

Week 2, Step 4. Tool: Spring 80/20 Shopping List (2 of 2).

SPRING/SUMMER 2014 (2)
WEEK 2 80/20 SHOPPING LIST | WWW.ULTIMATECLOSETGUIDE.COM

Style shaker

[C] refers to your 'Core Closet' pieces. [T] refers to your Trend Closet Pieces, and [B] refers to your Outfit Blueprint additions!

JEANS:
- [ ] [C] everyday wear with flats (boot-cut, slight flare)
- [ ] [C] everyday wear with heels (boot-cut, slight flare)
- [ ] [C] everyday skinny
- [ ] [C] dark wash skinny
- [ ] [C] dark wash bootcut/trouser cut
- [ ] [T] printed (floral, graphic) skinny
- [ ] [T] white denim
- [ ] [T] color skinny
- [ ] [B] _____
- [ ] [B] _____
- [ ] [B] _____
- [ ] [B] _____

PANTS:
- [ ] [C] neutral skinny pant (black, white, olive, grey)
- [ ] [C] summer shorts (neutral &/or printed)
- [ ] [C] classic black tailored pant
- [ ] [C] classic grey straight leg tailored pant
- [ ] [T] printed (skinny or drawstring)
- [ ] [T] white wide-leg pants
- [ ] [T] floral/pastel/pop-color skinny leg
- [ ] [T] drawstring (tuxedo stripe, print, or neutral)
- [ ] [B] _____
- [ ] [B] _____
- [ ] [B] _____
- [ ] [B] _____

SKIRTS:
- [ ] [C] classic pencil (neutrals: black and grey)
- [ ] [C] maxi (neutrals &/or solid color)
- [ ] [C] a-line (neutral black, grey, or solid color)
- [ ] [C] mini (depending on body type)
- [ ] [C] printed &/or metallic short/pencil skirt
- [ ] [T] pleated mid-length (color)
- [ ] [T] printed (silhouette best for your body type)
- [ ] [T] embellished, evening option
- [ ] [B] _____
- [ ] [B] _____
- [ ] [B] _____
- [ ] [B] _____

JEWELRY:
- [ ] [C] bracelets (gold & silver, everyday classic styles)
- [ ] [C] rings (gold & silver, everyday classic styles)
- [ ] [C] earrings (gold & silver, everyday studs/hoops)
- [ ] [C] necklaces (gold & silver, chain, classic)
- [ ] [C] cuff bracelets (rose gold, silver, small, classic)
- [ ] [T] statement jewelry (color, shape, all categories)
- [ ] [T] layered necklaces (color or metallic)
- [ ] [T] arm and/or ear cuffs
- [ ] [B] _____
- [ ] [B] _____
- [ ] [B] _____
- [ ] [B] _____

ACCESSORIES:
- [ ] [C] scarf (basic neutral or color)
- [ ] [C] sunglasses (classic, best fit for your face shape)
- [ ] [C] sarong (color or print)
- [ ] [C] classic two-piece suits (black, print, color)
- [ ] [C] classic one-piece suits (black, print, color)
- [ ] [T] printed scarf
- [ ] [T] oversized beach hat &/or sunglasses
- [ ] [T] retro bathing suit (one or two piece)
- [ ] [B] _____
- [ ] [B] _____
- [ ] [B] _____
- [ ] [B] _____

The BWIT Group. Copyright 2014. All rights reserved. TM pending

BRITTANY WITKIN

● **DON'T FORGET! VIEW THE TOOLKIT ON-LINE** ●

LINKS ON PAGES 119 & 120

page left blank
[so you can tear out this tool]

THE 30-DAY ULTIMATE CLOSET GUIDE

 # week 2 toolkit

Week 2, Step 6. Tool: Marathon Shopper Tip-sheet.

WEEK 1 MARATHON SHOPPER TIPSHEET | WWW.ULTIMATECLOSETGUIDE.COM   Style shaker

how to hack the shopping system:

1. Pick one central location that has all the stores you want to hit nearby. This is how you will avoid the whole 'running around town like a chicken with your head cut off' look.

2. If the location has a website, pre-shop on-line so you'll know what is in-store before you go. If you have the time call ahead to make sure the store has the styles you found on-line (many can send them over from other stores in the area if they're larger scale retailers/boutiques) and ask them to start a fitting room.

3. Bring your 80/20 Shopping List. For every item you need, assign a couple of stores within your 'designated shopping area' that is most likely (based on your pre-shopping) to have the item.

4. Map it out. Make a route (i.e. this store first, this store second, etc.) so you don't backtrack. You know what you need and where to get it. Time to harness your inner shopping ninja.

DON'T FORGET! VIEW THE TOOLKIT ON-LINE

LINKS ON PAGES 119 & 120

page left blank
[so you can tear out this tool]

closet notes

closet notes

closet notes

closet notes

BRITTANY WITKIN

{WEEK 1: Days 1 thru 7}

- make space -

"I'm making space for the unknown future to fill up my life with yet-to-come surprises." -Elizabeth Gilbert

AFTER WEEK 1 YOU WILL:

Be opening your doors every morning to a clutter-free, super-streamlined, and well-organized closet, filled only with items that will help you look your best.

THE WEEK 1 CLOSET TOOLKIT INCLUDES:

- ✗ The 30-Day Calendar
- ✗ The Closet Purge Cheat Sheet
- ✗ The Closet Overhaul Contract
- ✗ The Partner-in-Crime Invitation
- ✗ The Closet Re-Org Checklist
- ✗ The Closet Zen Card
- ✗ The Closet-to-Cash Link List
- ✗ The Closet Organization Inspiration List

TO HAVE ON HAND:

- ✗ printer
- ✗ four trash bags (heavy duty)
- ✗ my favorite hangers (link provided in Baby Prep Step 2)
- ✗ marker + sticky notes + tape
- ✗ phone (you'll use this to play music + also as a timer)

The Closet Overhaul is fundamentally important to the overall process not only because it helps you create space for amazing things to take place in your wardrobe, but also because it creates instant gratification that will act as a catalyst sending you into Week 2 with some serious styling momentum.

When you see your closet organized, clutter-free, and streamlined, you will immediately feel a shift and want to keep going. Pinky swear.

Internal Prep For External Transformation.

To shift and shake up your wardrobe you first have to shift and shake up your perspective. The next few paragraphs will help you do just that.

The most emotional part of the Ultimate Closet process happens straight out of the gate with Week 1 and the Closet Overhaul.

When you start letting go of things that have been collecting dust in your closet for awhile, it is very common to have a few mini (or not so mini) 'freak out' moments.

You can plan on feeling some sort of resistance along the way. It will happen, so you might as well accept that, and start to view it as a positive rather than a negative.

Think of the mini 'freak out' as a trigger for you to shift your focus from looking at what you are letting go of, to looking at what you are creating the space for.

Just think:

I am creating space for amazing things to happen.

That's it.

When the downward spiral starts to hit, it is your cue to pump the brakes and think or say:

I am creating space for amazing things to happen.

Say it until you mean it. Or just say it to get you over the Overhaul hump.

The truth? Here it is:

What's hanging in your closet is just 'stuff.'

There are stories behind some of this 'stuff.' There is a definite and undeniable emotional attachment to this 'stuff,' this I understand. You can (and should if it holds positive memories) keep the wedding dress, the worn-in college sweatshirt, jewelry your mom gave you (I do have a heart after all), but I'm going to ask that you limit yourself to keeping just a few (five to ten) items.

The past is the past, those stories have been told. Consider that it may be time to start writing some new stories.

Not to mention, I am willing to bet you good money that what you are letting go of will not be missed, especially if you can sell it and make a quick buck.

Let it go.

It's time to look forward, literally. Cue the 30-Day Calendar and my Baby Prep Steps…

THE 30-DAY ULTIMATE CLOSET GUIDE

DAY 1: MY PRE-OVERHAUL BABY PREP STEPS.

Time to take a few small steps to prepare you for Closet Overhaul day. Welcome to my Baby Prep Steps:

BABY PREP STEP 1: Go to the Week 1 Closet Toolkit at the beginning of the guide (page 12) and review the 30-Day Calendar. This is going to be the timeline that will get you to your Ultimate Closet in thirty days. You can reference the calendar in this guide as needed, or you can take it one step further, and add the deadlines you see on the 30-Day Calendar to your personal calendar so you stay on track. Preview below:

To edit it or enlarge it, you can access the 30-Day Calendar on-line by following this link: http://bit.ly/30daycalendar

BABY PREP STEP 2: You are going to want my all-time favorite hangers on hand when you start going through everything. They will not only save space, but also time. Nothing will slide off of them, no picking items back up and re-hanging.

Not to mention, having the same hangers for everything in your closet is one of the simplest (and most inexpensive) ways to visually organize things. Love that.

I won't go all Joan Crawford à la *Mommy Dearest* on you here. If you have a wire hanger or two in there, it is fine.

You can slowly work your way up to a full closet of what I'm sure will be your new favorite hangers, and you will see how something so small can have a huge impact.

If you already have them, you're ahead of the game (and/or one of my clients). These hangers will change your closet and life (yes, hangers can do that).

Follow this link to check them out:
http://bit.ly/besthangers

BABY PREP STEP 3: Make sure you have everything you own in your closet at the time of your Closet Overhaul. That means everything that is currently at the dry cleaners, in the laundry, in storage from last season, or has yet to be unpacked from your last trip, needs to be back in your closet in time for your Overhaul day.

BABY PREP STEP 4: Get your supplies in order ahead of time. Refer to the 'To Have on Hand' section at the beginning of this chapter and check everything off before you begin.

Baby Prep Steps, complete. Time for the big-girl steps…

{WEEK 1, STEPS 1-9}

(week 1, step 1)

DAY 1 CONTINUED: 30-DAY CALENDAR 101.

"What gets measured gets managed."–Peter Drucker

Go to your 30-Day Calendar in the Closet Toolkit to complete this step. I've already input calendar line items for you to work around. It's time to personalize your calendar. Plug in a starting month and dates so you can stay on track.

THE 30-DAY ULTIMATE CLOSET GUIDE

Done? Fabulous. You are now at the end of Week 1, Step 1 and per the calendar, this is your first stopping point. Feel free to keep going if you're up for it, or take a break and pick things up again tomorrow.

(week 1, step 2)

DAY 2: SCHEDULE YOUR CLOSET OVERHAUL.

Day two starts with blocking out and scheduling three to four hours on your 30-Day Calendar for your Closet Overhaul and Re-Org.

Go with what makes the most sense for your personal calendar. You can schedule this time all together in one block, or separate the time throughout your week.

	DAY 1	DAY 2	DAY 3	DAY 4	DAY 5	DAY 6	DAY 7
WEEK 1	*Complete Baby Prep Steps *Complete Week 1, Step 1	*Start Week 1, Steps 2-4	*Finish Week 1 Steps 2-4 *Read Week 1 Step 5 the day before the Closet Overhaul	*Closet Overhaul & Re-Org Place-holder *Week 1, Steps 6-8 (3-4 hours)	*Closet Overhaul & Re-Org Place-holder *Week 1, Steps 6-8 (3-4 hours)	*Closet Overhaul & Re-Org Place-holder *Week 1, Steps 6-8 (3-4 hours)	*Finish up Closet Overhaul *Complete Week 1, Step 9

Time is divided up as follows: two to three hours will go towards your Closet Overhaul leaving one hour, the last hour, to cover your closet Re-Org.

Depending on closet size and your level of emotional attachment to what you have in there, time allotment may differ from closet to closet. However, the rule of thumb is to stay as close to three to four hours for the entire Overhaul and Re-Org as possible. The faster, the better.

If you give yourself five hours, it will take five hours. You don't want to give yourself too much time to draw out decisions on what stays and what goes.

- **BRITT'S TIP:** Make a mental note that the day before you start your Closet Overhaul is when you should review Week 1, Step 5, the 'Day Before Your Overhaul' (page 55; you will also see this on your 30-Day Calendar as a reminder).

(week 1, step 3)

DAY 2 CONTINUED: SEND THE CLOSET CONTRACT.

It's about to get real. Ever heard of an accountability buddy? Well, this is a little bit like that.

The Closet Overhaul Contract was created so you don't have to go it alone (sometimes it takes a village, or just one amazing friend). For Step 3, you will send out the Closet Contract to a close, supportive friend you can depend on to help you keep your Closet Overhaul commitment.

It takes five minutes and will be your secret motivational weapon for Week 1.

Cut out the contract from the Week 1 Closet Toolkit (page 13) at the beginning of the guide, date it, sign it, and send it off. Preview below:

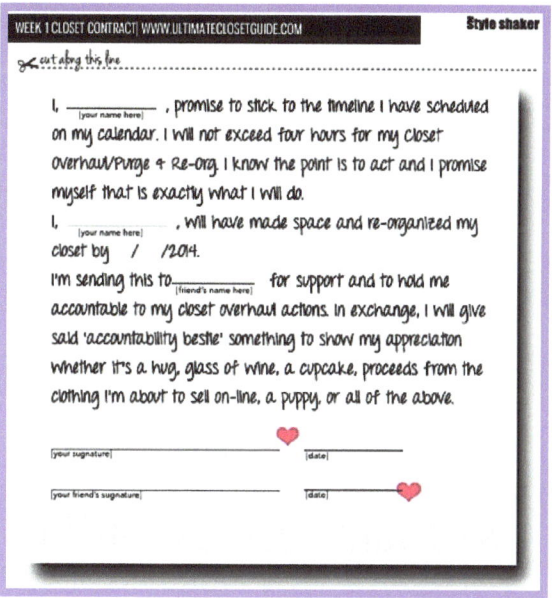

Would you rather send it in an email? Follow the link below to find the email template and send away. Once you have sign-off from your friend, move ahead to the next step.

Here's the link:

http://bit.ly/closetcontract

(week 1, step 4)

DAY 2 CONTINUED: TURN IT INTO A PARTY. [OPTIONAL]

If you're scheduling your Closet Overhaul for one block of time, why not turn it into a party right?

I've created the Partner-In-Crime Closet Invitation to make the party-planning process simple for you. Preview below:

You can find it in the Week 1 Closet Toolkit at the beginning of this guide (page 15).

Choose your invitees carefully! You have a time limit and will need someone who can have fun, stay focused, and above all, someone who will tell you like it is.

Think of the friend you always go shopping with when you want an honest opinion. That is the name you want to write on the invitation. That is your P.I.C (Partner-In-Crime)!

She/he is going to keep you honest and help you get to where you want to be. She/he may also be the person you just sent your Closet Contract to in the previous step.

You can tear/cut out the Invitation (page 15), personalize it, and send away! Or, you can follow this link to find the email template that you can copy and paste if you prefer going that route: http://bit.ly/closetinvitation

(week 1, step 5)

THE DAY BEFORE YOUR OVERHAUL.

You have scheduled your Closet Overhaul on your 30-Day Calendar. Check.

You have your Closet Contract signed. Check.

You have sent out the P.I.C. (Partner-In-Crime) invite. Check. Now I'm going to quickly share with you how I approach a Closet Overhaul. Read this next section and incorporate anything you find helpful as you head into your very own Closet Overhaul day!

Industry-Insider Tips: How I Go Through A Closet.

I start by visually dividing a closet into three sections (you can also do this by placing your sticky notes strategically throughout as a visual marker if that works better for you). Dividing things into three large areas allows me to stay focused and on track.

I usually get through (i.e. review and decide whether it stays or goes) everything hanging in about two and a half hours (closet size can affect this, so it's important to be realistic and not get discouraged). If you have a large walk-in closet (first of all, congratulations) give yourself a little more time.

Following my review of what is hanging up (clothing), I go straight into accessories in this order: shoes, bags, scarves/belts, and finally jewelry. The four trash bags (you will learn about this in a minute) are always nearby so I don't have to go too far to start filling them up.

Also, I try to spend a very limited time on anything that falls into the 'active wear' category. If you have workout clothing you haven't worn in over six months, let it go (refer to the Closet Purge Cheat Sheet in the next step, Step 6, for more quick questions you can ask to get you over the fence when you need to make a decision).

Unless you are a yoga instructor/Pilates teacher/trainer this will not be a large part of your daily wardrobe routine, and as such, should not take up too much of your energy. If you are one of the above, you are going to need to go through this section as you would everything else.

The good news is, you're in great shape, so you can handle it!

(week 1, step 6)

CLOSET OVERHAUL DAY: THE FIRST 2-3 HOURS.

Welcome to your Closet Overhaul Day! Before you begin going through the items in your closet, review and follow the four small prep-steps listed below (this should take under thirty minutes).

1. PREP YOUR BAGS- Grab a box of super-durable trash bags (the last thing you need to deal with is a trash bag explosion).

Pull out four bags. Here's what they will be for:
1. Donate
2. Sell
3. Trash
4. Hangers

Grab some colorful sticky notes (you have extra tape on hand for reinforcement, so you don't see sticky notes scattered across the floor of your closet) and a marker.

Label your trash bags accordingly and place them nearby so they are ready to go.

2. PREP THE TIMER- Set your timer for the halfway mark based on the time you've allotted for your Overhaul (i.e. set to two hours if you have allotted four hours for the entire Overhaul).

After the timer goes off, stop and look at your progress. This is going to help keep you on track.

Adjust accordingly (speed up if need be) so you can make it through with the remaining time you have on the clock. Tick, tock.

- **BRITT'S TIP:** Keep in mind, if you have scheduled your Closet Overhaul in multiple blocks of time, once you reach your time limit, you will place a sticky note (add extra tape here, you don't want to lose your place) on the hanger where you left off. This will be your starting point for your next round.

THE 30-DAY ULTIMATE CLOSET GUIDE

3. PREP FOR KEEPING YOUR CLOSET COOL- First, have your Closet Zen Card nearby. You can find it in the Week 1 Closet Toolkit at the beginning of this guide (page 19).

If/when you get overwhelmed, pull that little card out and read it to bring things back into perspective. Preview below:

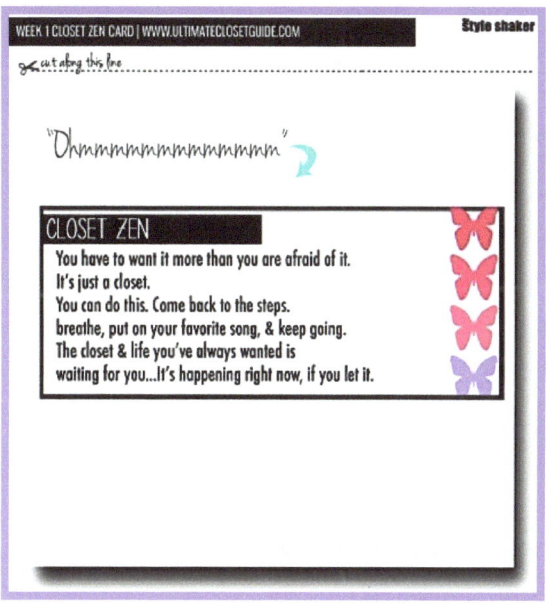

You also have your mantra from the beginning of the chapter to fall back on. Here it is if you need another reminder:

I am creating space for amazing things to happen.

Both the Closet Zen card and your mantra will help pull you

out of a panic by taking a little bit of the emotion out of the situation, all so you can make some quick decisions.

Second, find the Closet Purge Cheat Sheet in the Week 1 Closet Toolkit at the beginning of the guide (page 17).

The Cheat Sheet will be your go-to tool when you get stuck on an item. Preview below:

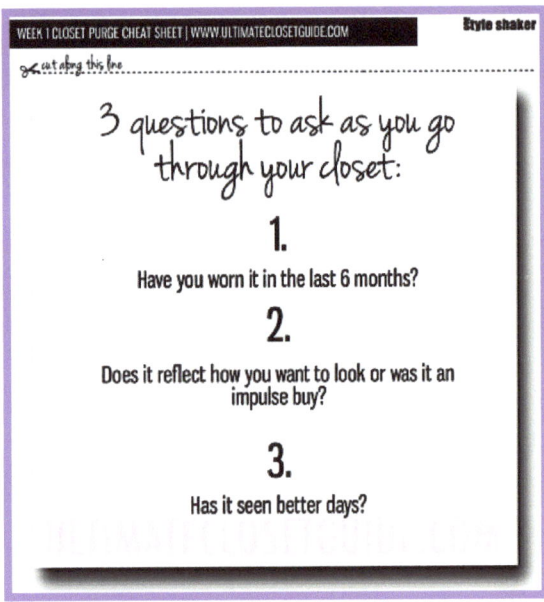

The questions listed on this Cheat Sheet are the exact same questions I use with my private clients during the Closet Overhaul process and they work like a charm.

How To Use The Cheat Sheet.

If you can't decide whether something should stay or go, ask yourself the three questions on the Cheat Sheet, in the order they are listed, and you will get to a decision. Guaranteed. It starts with question number one:

1.
Have you worn it in the last six months?

Usually, the first question, 'have you worn it in the last six months' will make the decision a quick and painless one for you. If it has been over six months since you have worn something, and it is not a seasonal item (i.e. shorts) then it is time to **let it go**. If you have worn it in the past six months, but you are still unsure, go to the second question…

2.
Does it reflect how you want to look?

If the item is not in-line with the vision you have of your updated look or current lifestyle (i.e. you have a closet filled with black suits and you left the corporate world two years ago), **let it go**. Still unsure, move along to the next question on the Cheat Sheet…

3.
Has it seen better days?

If you have a favorite item you wear all the time, but it has seen better days (i.e. you can't hide the holes/pilling/discoloration anymore), it is time to **let it go**.

But before you do, if this favorite item works for your body type and lifestyle (you can always ask for the opinion of a friend, or your Partner-In-Crime on this), you may just need a new version of it. If that is the case, label it 'Needs Replacement' or 'NR' with a sticky note, put it to the side in your closet, and move on.

- **BRITT'S TIP:** In Week 2, Step 4, you will add this 'NR' item to your 80/20 Shopping List under the appropriate category. Hold on to it for now (but yes, you will need to pull it out of heavy outfit rotation).

- **BRITT'S TIP:** If you are making your Overhaul into a party, now would be a great time to leverage your Partner-In-Crime. Should you still be unsure about whether an item stays or goes after you have asked the three questions on your Cheat Sheet, nothing helps make a decision faster than trying it on and getting your Partner-In-Crime's honest opinion. Don't have a P.I.C in your closet with you? Send a quick pic of yourself wearing the item in question to the friend (accountability buddy) you sent your Closet Contract to. Ask for a quick thumbs up or thumbs down, and you're ready to move on to the next item!

4. LAST, BUT NOT LEAST, PREP & SET THE MOOD- Great music is a serious mood lifter. This we all know. Have an energizing playlist going during your Overhaul to set the tone.

It also helps to have your favorite snacks on hand (low blood sugar does not a pleasant Closet Overhaul make), and hydration is key to keeping energy levels up, so keep some water nearby.

If you decide to turn your Overhaul into a party, there is nothing wrong with having a cocktail or two at this point.

I'm going to recommend a two drink maximum for this. You can go big once Week 1 is over. Cheers to that!

Ok, go ahead with your Overhaul!

Once you have completed Step 6, it's time for Step 7, the other half of this fashion equation, The Re-Org!

(week 1, step 7)

CLOSET OVERHAUL DAY, PART 2: THE RE-ORG.

The Overhaul is complete! Your trash bags are full and ready to go. Now that you can see what is in your cleaned out closet (love that), it's time to organize what you have left.

Head to the Week 1 Closet Toolkit at the beginning of the guide and cut out your Closet Re-Org Checklist (page 21).

The Re-Org will play an instrumental role in simplifying how you get dressed everyday.

You're about to turn your closet into a well-oiled, outfit-making machine. Ready? Preview below:

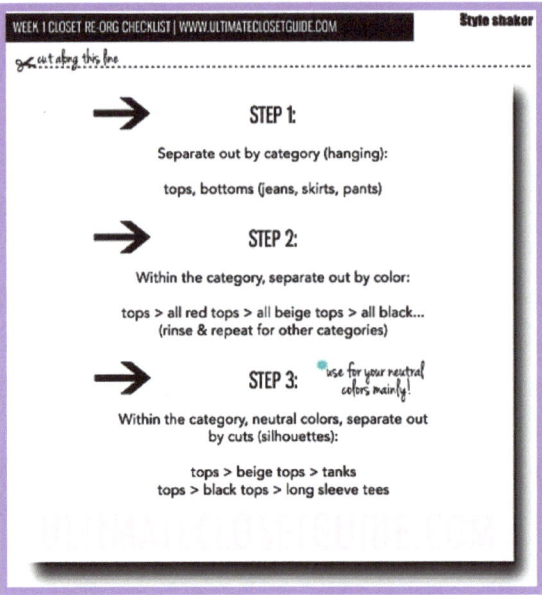

First, you will want to get everything you can on a hanger (preferably the hangers you bought during Baby Prep Step 2, page 48). Knits, however, you will want to keep folded so they don't stretch out.

The goal here is simple: you need to be able to see what you're working with and hanging everything up will accomplish that in a snap.

Once everything is officially up where you can see it, begin the Closet Re-Org. Just as before, set your timer halfway (thirty minutes; you have an hour total for this).

Follow the three steps on the Closet Re-Org Checklist to divide everything out accordingly.

One additional tip is to keep the shoes and bags you wear the most front and forward. They get far more wardrobe 'play' than other items and as such, should be easily accessible.

Go for it!

(week 1, step 8)

EXTRAS: WEEK 1 GOODIES.

Never Ending Closet Organization Inspiration.

If you want to check out more brilliant DIY Closet Organization ideas (like using foam board to organize dresser drawers or hanging up clipboards on a wall to keep your necklaces detangled and looking fabulous, etc.), check out the Closet Organization Inspiration List by following the link below: http://bit.ly/closetinspiration

Take a look, get inspired, but be careful not to go too far down the rabbit hole and lose all sense of time. I know, it is tempting (and addictive), but you have thirty days so let's keep going…

One Person's 'Sell' Pile, Is Another Person's Treasure.

As for the leftovers that made it into your 'Sell' bag, if you are going to take the time to go through the Closet Overhaul, might as well make some extra cash while you are at it right?

My Closet Into Cash List covers a few select websites that will help you sell what you are letting go of. Follow the below link to see the list of sites I've tested successfully and continue to use for selling items from my own closet:

http://bit.ly/closettocash

(week 1, step 9)

DAY 7: CLEAR IT OUT.

Almost there!

I recommend moving quickly when it comes to clearing out the bags you filled up (Donate, Sell, Hangers, Trash) during your Closet Overhaul.

The longer they sit around, the more wavering you will do on items you initially let go of.

Drop them off at a donation location, schedule a pick-up, list them on-line, bring them to a consignment store, toss them, whatever you need to do to make it happen, do it. You want to start off Week 2 with a clean wardrobe slate!

And with that I'll say…

Congratulations!

Week 1 is complete!

This is major.

Take a moment to reflect and relax before you head into Week 2. Don't forget, you can share your Week 1 stories, pics & more by following the below link to connect & inspire others!

Here's the link:

http://bit.ly/tellyourclosetstory

{WEEK 2: Days 8 thru 14}

- the outfit blueprint -

"Your vision of where or who you want to be is the greatest asset you have" –Paul Arden

AFTER WEEK 2 YOU WILL:

Know exactly what you will be wearing for every occasion on your calendar next week. And if that weren't enough, you will also have created a personalized 80/20 Shopping List that will be the one and only list you'll need this season to take the stress out of shopping.

THE WEEK 2 CLOSET TOOLKIT INCLUDES:

✗ The Outfit Planner Template & Worksheet

✗ Direct access to my Four Outfit Blueprint Lookbooks

✗ Links to TheStyleShaker.com 'Body Type Styling Guide'

✗ The 80/20 Shopping List: Fall and Spring 2014

✗ Access to my Core and Trend Shopping Lists

✗ The On-line Shopping 'Hit List'

✗ The 'Marathon Shopper' Tip-Sheet

TO HAVE ON HAND:

✗ printer

✗ scissors

✗ tape

✗ highlighter & pen

Your closet is squeaky clean, you've gone all 'wardrobe-ninja' on everything, and you are ready to take the next step. Fabulous. Welcome, to Week 2!

It's time to create your Outfit Blueprints and pull together your 80/20 Shopping List…

OUTFIT BLUEPRINTS: THE BREAKDOWN.

The Outfit Blueprint is exactly what it sounds like. You're about to create a 'blueprint' for every occasion on your calendar. Think of it as a style-template that will show you how to update your look and simplify getting dressed every day.

The Outfit Blueprints will also offer some direction on what items you may want to consider adding to your 80/20 Shopping List (more on that in a bit). The goal here is to keep it simple, so I've split up the Outfit Blueprints into four main types, or occasions (below).

During the week (depending on your lifestyle) you are bound to wear an outfit that fits into at least two of the following Outfit Blueprint Types:

1. **DAY/POLISHED:** business meetings/lunches, corporate work, freelance work, school functions, luncheons, interviews, etc.

2. **DAY/CASUAL:** weekend brunches, running errands, going to class, picnics, lunch with friends/family, picking up the kids, etc.

3. **EVENING/DRESSY:** cocktail parties, date nights, black-tie events, semi- formal events, holiday parties, gallery openings, plays, etc.

4. **EVENING/CASUAL:** dinner with friends/family, running errands, movie nights, live music events, drinks with friends, etc.

{WEEK 2, STEPS 1-6}

(week 2, step 1)

DAY 8: FILL-IN THE OUTFIT PLANNER.

Now that you know what the four main Outfit Blueprint Types are, it's time to see where they fit into your personal calendar. Everyone will have a different balance when it comes to the four Outfit Blueprint Types. Some of us go to dinner all the time. Some of us get out to dinner once in a blue moon. Some of us work a nine-to-five job, some of us work from home. You get the picture. Your Outfit Planner Worksheet will be a direct reflection of you personal calendar. You can find the Outfit Planner Template in the Week 2 Closet Toolkit at the beginning of the guide (page 23). Preview below:

1. PENCIL IN YOUR OCCASION- Starting with Sunday (next week) enter what you have planned for both daytime and evening occasions on to your Outfit Planner worksheet.

See where to enter this information on the Outfit Planner worksheet by referring to the image below. You will enter your occasion on top of the line, where the pink arrows are pointing:

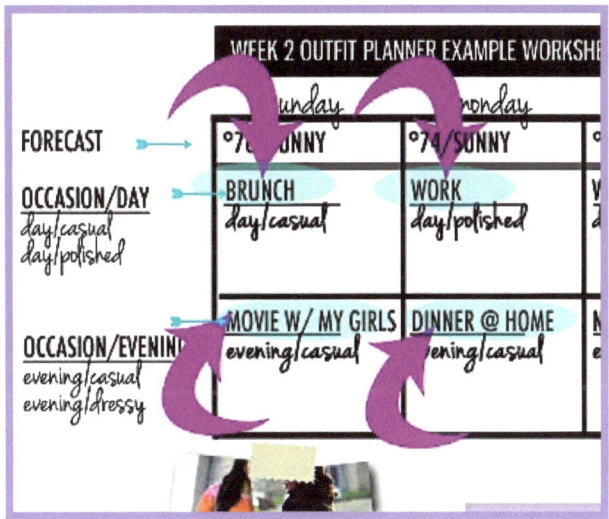

- **BRITT'S TIP:** Whether you're running errands or going to a brunch during the day, pencil it in on your Outfit Planner. The only occasions you can leave out are those that don't involve you being out in public (i.e. a night in at home wearing sweats). Not everyone does something every day/night on their social calendar, I get it. Mark those non-outfit times with an 'n/a' to keep it simple.

Continue entering this information for the rest of the week.

- **BRITT'S TIP:** If you have several things going on during the day, but can wear the same outfit for all of them (you can always switch up a look with a change of shoe that you cleverly keep in your oversized tote), lump those into one occasion, 'Errands,' or, 'Meetings,' and so on.

You can see an example of what a completed Outfit Planner looks like by reviewing the Outfit Planner Example in the Week 2, Closet Toolkit found at the beginning of the guide (page 25).

2. PENCIL IN THE CORRESPONDING OUTFIT BLUEPRINT TYPE- Next you will enter the Outfit Blueprint Type under the occasion you just entered on the Planner.

Remember, you have four to choose from: Day/Polished, Day/Casual, Evening/Dressy, and Evening/Casual.

These Outfit Blueprint Types correspond to Lookbooks I have created for you to use as you pull inspiration for the week. More on that in a minute.

Enter the corresponding Outfit Blueprint Type according to the occasion you have on your Outfit Planner (i.e. your Sunday brunch calls for a 'Daytime/Casual' Outfit Blueprint Type/outfit).

See an example of how to do this step below…

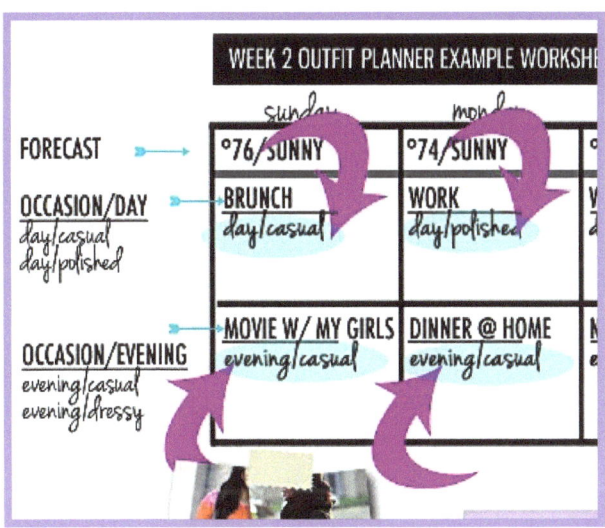

Enter the Outfit Blueprint Type below the line, where the pink arrows are pointing.

Continue this for the rest of the week until your Planner is full and looks similar to the Outfit Planner Example you found in your Week 2 Closet Toolkit (see on the next page):

![Week 2 Outfit Planner Example Worksheet]

3. HOW'S THE WEATHER? - I've also created a spot for you to update the weather for the week. It is just an optional add-on, but it comes in handy when you start to plan out your outfits. Go ahead and fill in the forecast for the week if you'd like.

(week 2, step 2)

DAY 8 CONTINUED: FIND YOUR LOOK INSPIRATION.

Now that your first Outfit Planner worksheet is completely filled in, it's time to find seven daytime and seven evening (adjust accordingly to the number of occasions you have on your Planner) looks that will guide and inspire you to create updated outfits for the week ahead.

I have an entire library of looks, separated out by Outfit Blueprint Type, that you will use for this step. You can access this looks library (otherwise known as The Lookbooks) on-line by following the link provided below:

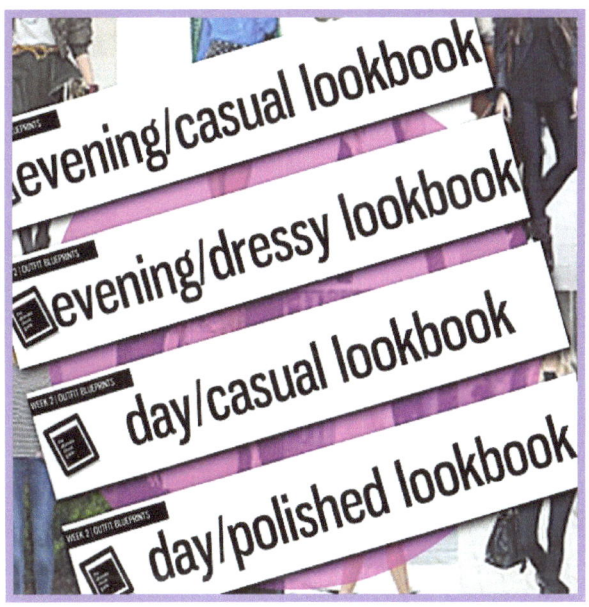

http://bit.ly/thelookbooks

Open all four Lookbooks on your computer and refer back to your Outfit Planner.

Start with your first occasion on Sunday. What Outfit Blueprint Type do you have listed on there? I will use Daytime/Casual as an example.

Now that you know what Outfit Blueprint Type you're looking for, head over to the corresponding (in this case Daytime/Casual) Lookbook on-line, and scroll through to find a look you would like to try/use for inspiration.

• **BRITT'S TIP:** Remember to keep an open mind and have fun with this! Think inspiration, not imitation, and try not to get caught up in the details or negative 'self-talk.'

You *can* (and will with my help) pull these looks off (not every look is for every body, but go towards the looks that instantly resonate with you, whether you think you can pull them off or not).

My job is to show you how to do just that. All you need to do is pick a look that you love!

You will take pieces from each look and apply them to your own wardrobe. **I suggest focusing less on *what* is pictured and more on *how* it is being worn.**

Once you have found your favorite look for that first day and occasion, print it out. Instructions covering how to print are here: http://bit.ly/thelookbooks

Two Things To Consider As You Search For Inspiration Looks:

1. For the first week, opt for looks that include one to two items that are similar to something you currently have in your closet. You are just starting to build-up your wardrobe, so working with what you already own is a big part of the first Outfit Planning round.

2. You can put different looks on your Outfit Planner for each day, OR you can copy a look from one day to another and make it different with a small adjustment that could be as simple as the addition of an accessory/jewelry, the ommission of a layer of clothing, swapping a heel for a flat, etc. One small change can transform an entire look.

Go ahead and repeat this process (find the look, print the look out) for each day and occasion on next week's Outfit Planner.

You will be left with a stack of updated looks! Next up, compile the pages of looks, putting them in order of days of the week, and attach them to the updated Outfit Planner worksheet.

You can tape them on, re-size the images to print them out smaller and glue them on, or just staple the packet of looks together and clip them onto the one Outfit Planner worksheet (the last option is how I do it).

The goal is to have one stack you can easily carry with you into, or keep inside of, your closet.

(week 2, step 3)

DAY 8 CONTINUED: BODY TYPE CONSIDERATIONS.

If you happen to get hung up on what looks and silhouettes work best for your body type, or if you are still wondering what body type you are, check out the Body Type Guide I created for my clients.

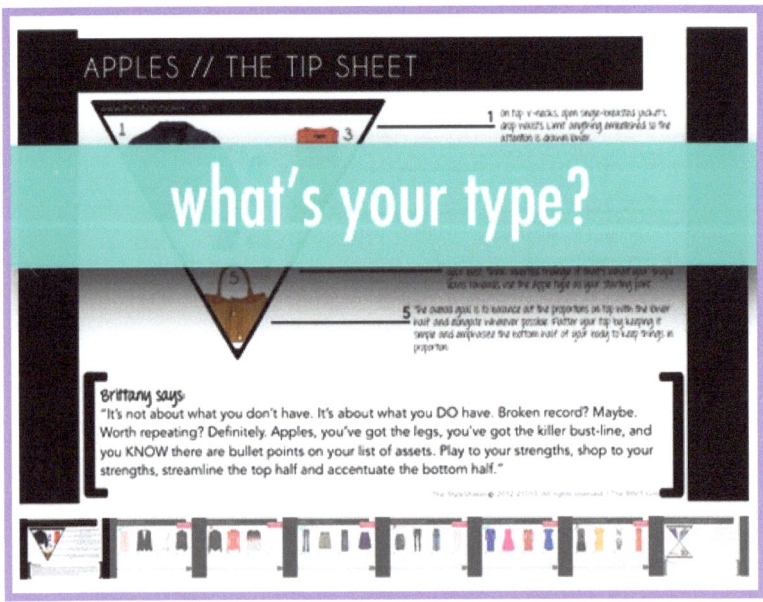

This guide will show you what silhouettes work (and don't work) for each body type, as well as how to define what body type you fall into.

- **BRITT'S TIP:** We are all a hybrid when it comes to body types. The good news is, we all tend to lean more towards one type than another.

Take your cue from whatever your most dominant feature is (larger on top, larger on bottom, curvy on top and bottom, curve-free, etc.) and go with the body type that speaks to that shape most.

The guide will walk you through the rest! Follow this link to start reading: http://bit.ly/bodytypeguide

(week 2, step 4)

DAY 9: YOUR CLOSET BASELINE, THE 80/20 SHOPPING LIST.

At this point, you have your Outfit Planner all set for next week. You will be creating the updated looks on your Planner using what is already in your cleaned out closet. To complete the Planner looks, you may also need to fill in some 'wardrobe holes' with new items. Enter: The 80/20 Shopping List!

Go to the Week 2, Closet Toolkit in the beginning of the guide and check out the 80/20 Shopping List (pages 27-33). Previews on the next page:

THE 30-DAY ULTIMATE CLOSET GUIDE

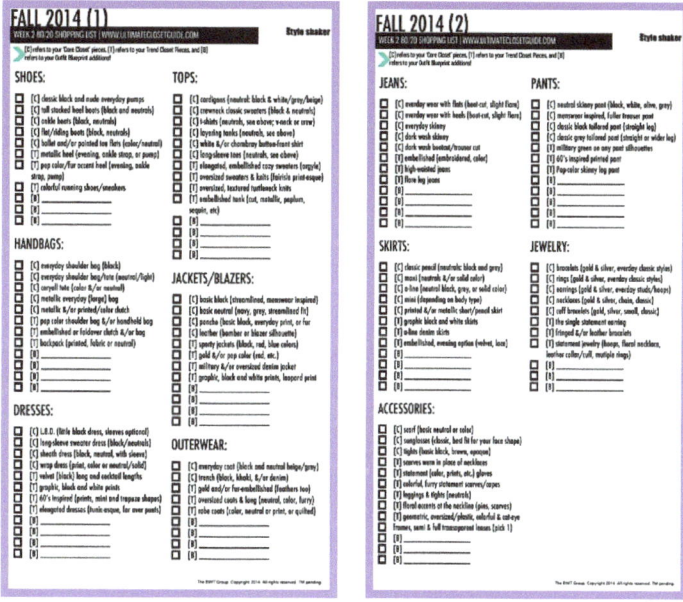

You can download the larger digital version by following this link: http://bit.ly/8020shoppinglist

What Is The 80/20 Shopping List?

The 80/20 Shopping List is a direct reflection of what you'll find in most Ultimate Closets (and is split out according to season).

Around 80% of an Ultimate Closet is filled with 'Core' pieces (i.e. your workhorse, investment pieces, a.k.a. the essentials) leaving the remaining 20% to be filled with 'Trend' pieces (fashion-forward picks updated seasonally; usually with a heavy focus on accessories).

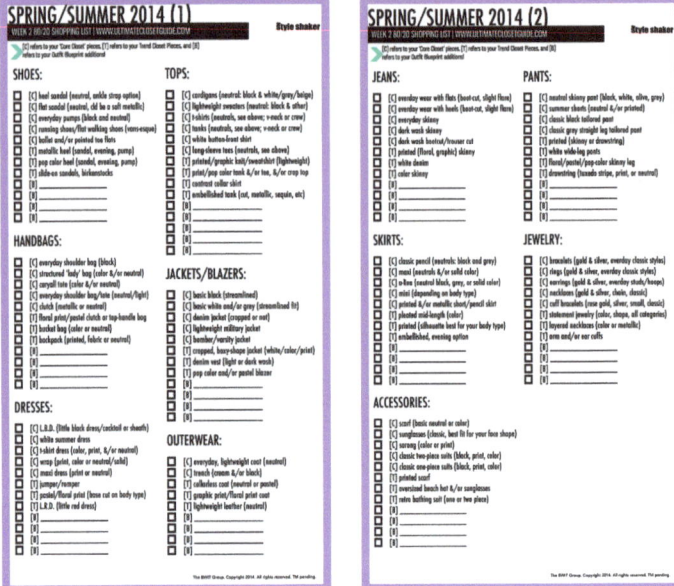

The closet equation looks a little something like this:

80% CORE + 20% TREND (PERSONALIZED TO YOUR LIFESTYLE) = YOUR HAPPY PLACE/ULTIMATE CLOSET

The percentages do not have to be approximate. This is not an exact science, as an Ultimate Closet is always evolving.

The 80/20 Shopping List gives you a bit of direction that will help you keep your high-functioning wardrobe as efficient and balanced as possible, whatever the season.

It is also the *only* list you will need in your hands for a fail-proof experience every time you go shopping (in-store or on-line).

Let's Review The 80/20 Shopping List Lingo:

- Where you see [C] on the Shopping List, I'm referring to Core items.
- Where you see [T] I'm referring to Trend items.
- Where you see [B] I'm referring to Outfit Blueprint items.

Simple, right? Moving along…

Bonus Round.

So what does a 'Core' item look like? And what does a 'Trend' item look like? Good questions. Rather than me telling you, I've created two shopping lists that will show you what I'm referring to when I use those two terms. Links below…

The CORE (the essentials) list is here:
http://bit.ly/coreitems

The TREND (here one season, gone the next) list is here:
http://bit.ly/trenditems

Putting The 80/20 Shopping List To Work.

Now that you have your 80/20 List in hand, it's time for a little closet cross-reference.

First, check off anything on the shopping list that you already see inside of your closet. No need to shop for it, you already have it!

If you check off an item that you think may need to be

replaced soon. Put that item on the 80/20 Shopping List as you will probably need to buy a replacement soon. Speaking of…

Don't Forget! The 'Needs Replacement' or 'NR' Group From Your Overhaul.

Remember the pieces you marked 'Needs Replacement' from Week 1 (page 62)? Make sure those are added to your 80/20 Shopping List as well, whether they're part of the Core group, Trend group, or just add-ons.

(week 2, step 5)

DAY 9 CONTINUED: OUTFIT BLUEPRINT ADDITIONS TO THE 80/20 LIST.

	DAY 8	DAY 9	DAY 10	DAY 11	DAY 12	DAY 13	DAY 14
WEEK 2	*Complete Week 2, Steps 1-3	*Complete Week 2, Steps 4 and 5	*Week 2, Step 6: ON-LINE Shoppers start shopping for delivery next week	*Week 2, Step 6: IN-STORE, schedule shopping ON-LINE shopping cont.	*Week 2, Step 6: Shopping placeholders, ON-LINE & IN-STORE	*Week 2, Step 6: Shopping placeholders, ON-LINE & IN-STORE	*Week 2, Step 6: Finalize shopping trip in-store, and on-line try-on/returns
	DAY 15	DAY 16	DAY 17	DAY 18	DAY 19	DAY 20	DAY 21

Next, you will go through the looks (now on your Outfit Planner) you found and printed out from the Lookbooks earlier (Week 2, Step 2).

Each look will have a few main components to it. A top, a bottom (unless it's a dress), and accessories (shoes, bags, jewelry, scarves, etc.).

For the first look, notice the first outfit component (top, dress, etc.). On your 80/20 Shopping List under the corresponding category (top, dress, etc.) do you see a line/space for it?

- If you do see it on the 80/20 Shopping List, and it is checked off, that means it (or something similar to it) is already in your closet. Move on to the next component in the printed inspirational look.

- If you do see it on the 80/20 Shopping List, and it is unchecked, highlight or circle that item to prioritize it for when you go shopping next.

- If you don't see it as an option on your 80/20 Shopping List, write the item in the appropriate category on empty lines following '[B]' and highlight this item to prioritize it for when you go shopping next.

Walk through an example on the next page…

Example: Following taking inventory of your closet (Week 2, Step 4), on the Outfit Planner, you start with your Sunday inspiration look (printed out earlier). One component in that look is a black ankle boot.

You go over to the 'Shoes' category in your 80/20 Shopping List and see 'ankle boot' listed. It is un-checked which means, you don't already own a basic black ankle boot. You can also see it is a Core piece. Highlight that line to prioritize it on your 80/20 Shopping List.

Next you move on to the next component in the inspiration look, the jacket, and so on…

Continue this process with all inspiration looks you have printed out and attached to your Outfit Planner. By the end, your 80/20 Shopping List will be updated and ready to go!

How To Prioritize Your List.

The Core, or essential items on your 80/20 Shopping List that are left unchecked, should always come first. Focusing on these will help you achieve a solid wardrobe foundation.

After that, you can focus on the Blueprint items you will need to create the looks on your Outfit Planner next week. Trend items are lowest in priority, although there may be some overlap between Trend and Blueprint picks (which is a bonus really). See below:

1. CORE
2. BLUEPRINT
3. TREND

- **BRITT'S TIP:** Use your creativity here. When you can shop for one item that falls into the Blueprint and Trend category (it doesn't have to be exact), do it.

It isn't about buying more. It's about using more of what you already own to create updated looks. This is why I suggested leveraging Lookbook inspiration outfits that lend themselves to what is already in your closet earlier. This will also help you keep that happy balance of 80/20 in your Ultimate Closet.

(week 2, step 6)

DAYS 10-14: THREE DIFFERENT SHOPPING APPROACHES.

- **BRITT'S TIP:** Make sure you review the outline on your 30-Day calendar (page 12) at this point, screen-shot below. Timing will be critical with on-line deliveries.

WEEK 2	DAY 8	DAY 9	DAY 10	DAY 11	DAY 12	DAY 13	DAY 14
	*Complete Week 2, Steps 1-3	*Complete Week 2, Steps 4 and 5	*Week 2, Step 6: ON-LINE Shoppers start shopping for delivery next week	*Week 2, Step 6: IN-STORE, schedule shopping ON-LINE shopping cont.	*Week 2, Step 6: Shopping placeholders, ON-LINE & IN-STORE	*Week 2, Step 6: Shopping placeholders, ON-LINE & IN-STORE	*Week 2, Step 6: Finalize shopping trip in-store, and on-line try-on/returns
	DAY 15	DAY 16	DAY 17	DAY 18	DAY 19	DAY 20	DAY 21

Your 80/20 Shopping List is now filled in and highlighted.

Time to review your shopping options (note that you don't have to pick one or the other; go with what works best for you):

OPTION 1, ON-LINE SHOPPERS- Since you're doing the majority of your shopping on-line, it's important that you buy a.s.a.p. to stay on your 30-Day Ultimate Closet track. The 30-Day calendar lines up all of the deadlines for you so you will have all of your high priority items on your 80/20 List in time for creating next week's outfits.

In order to help you find what you need, I'm giving you access to my edited 'Hit List' of on-line shopping websites (only websites with speedy processing and delivery times made the list).

Note: On some websites you will need to buy a minimum to qualify for free shipping (I also steered clear of websites that charged heavily for return shipping; no one site is perfect, but these are some of the best options out there).

Preview below:

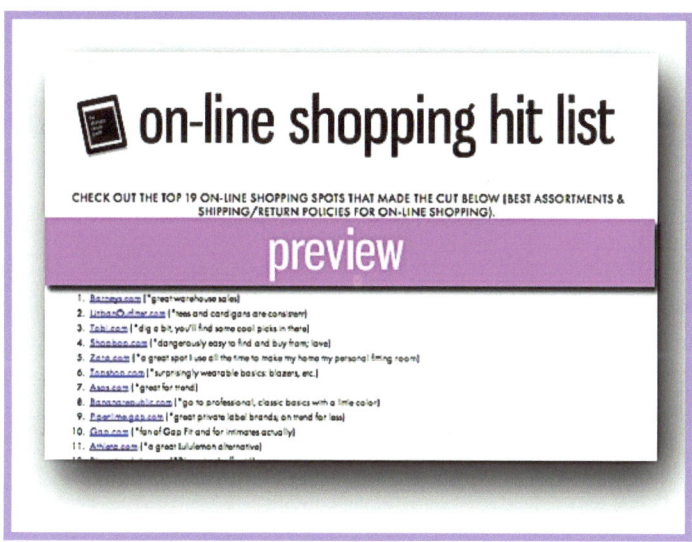

Follow the link below to access the On-line Shopping Hit List: http://bit.ly/shoppinghitlist

If you don't feel up to going through the Hit List, you can go straight to TheStyleShaker.com Shopping List updated weekly, and shop the featured products by category. The digging is done for you.

Follow this link to access it:

http://bit.ly/styleshakershoppinglist

Another quick time-saving step you can take when shopping on-line is to buy two sizes at once. It will cost more up front, but in the end, will save you precious time.

Also, if you time it correctly (around your billing statement and on-line processing times) you may be able to (I personally do this all the time) send your return back and be credited before your next billing cycle.

Finally, you may not have the time to deal with deliveries and returns, but other people do (if you are willing to pay them a small fee). There are some amazing on-line services (couriers and task-masters) out there in select cities that are built for just this kind of thing. Remember, keep it simple!

OPTION 2, IN-STORE SHOPPERS- There's in-store shopping and then there's *in-store* shopping.

Why not make your shopping trip a one-stop-shop kind of event since time is of the essence?

You can find the Marathon Shopper Tip-sheet in the Week 2 Closet Toolkit located at the beginning of the guide (page 35).

See how to take your shopping-ninja skills to the next level by following the steps on the tip-sheet. Preview on the next page…

THE 30-DAY ULTIMATE CLOSET GUIDE

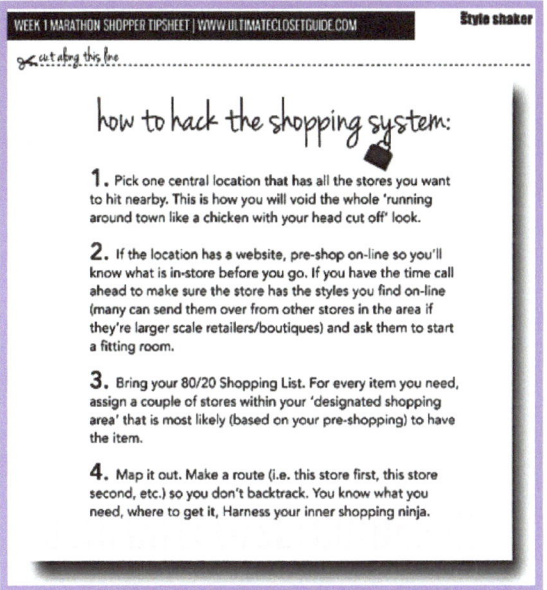

Or, if you want to slow the pace down a bit on your shopping day(s), you can take a cue from your Closet Overhaul and turn this into a party. Bring along your Partner-In-Crime (your honest friend in the fitting room) and make a day of it!

• **BRITT'S TIP:** The one thing I'm going to suggest you do no matter what, is **try everything on**. If you see something you like, but aren't sure, try it on. Always.

If you never try it on, you'll never know.

• **BRITT'S TIP:** As you add new pieces to your wardrobe, make sure you check off those items and update your 80/20 Shopping list.

Now that you have everything you need to get your 'shop-on' go for it! During Week 3 you get to put the Outfit Planner to work…

BRITTANY WITKIN

{WEEK 3: Days 15 thru 21}

"The only person you are destined to become is the person you decide to be." –Ralph Waldo Emerson

AFTER WEEK 3 YOU WILL:

Have completed your first week of knowing what to wear for every occasion on your calendar (thank you, Outfit Planner). At the end of Week 3 you will also be prepared to do the same thing next week.

THE WEEK 3 CLOSET TOOLKIT INCLUDES:

✗ Reference all tools from the Week 2 Closet Toolkit at the beginning of this guide

TO HAVE ON HAND:

✗ Your 30-Day Calendar

✗ Your 80/20 Shopping List

✗ Last Week's Outfit Planner

✗ A new Outfit Planner Template (to fill out this week)

✗ tape

✗ scissors

✗ printer

You've put a dent in your 80/20 Shopping List and can now start creating (and wearing) the looks on your Outfit Planner.

Welcome to Week 3!

The Ultimate Closet is a living, breathing thing. This week is all about putting that first Outfit Planner to the test and working out any kinks as your personal styling process continues to evolve.

The goal is to keep the momentum going. Not only will you be wearing your updated looks, but you will also be planning out next week's outfits.

{WEEK 3, STEPS 1-4}

(week 3, step 1)

DAY 15: THE TRAINING WHEELS COME OFF.

Time to take another look at the 30-Day Calendar (page 12). On it you will see a couple of line-items at the start of Week 3. See a preview below:

	DAY 15	DAY 16	DAY 17	DAY 18	DAY 19	DAY 20	DAY 21
WEEK 3	*Complete Week 3, Step 1	*Use Outfit Planner #1 *Follow-up on shopping list where needed	*Use Outfit Planner #1 *Follow-up on shopping list where needed	*Use Outfit Planner #1 *Steps 2 and 3	*Use Outfit Planner #1 *Follow-up on shopping list where needed	*Use Outfit Planner #1 *Follow-up on shopping list where needed	*Complete Week 3, Step 4 *Follow-up on shopping list where needed
	DAY 22	DAY 23	DAY 24	DAY 25	DAY 26	DAY 27	DAY 28

By Day 15, you should be finishing up the shopping you did last week. You may not be able to get absolutely everything you need. That is fine.

Remember: It's not about changing the 'what' or the contents of your closet, as much as it is about changing up 'how' you use what you already own.

Next, you're going to take what you have in your closet, along with your latest shopping list additions, and use the Outfit Planner you pulled together last week to start creating your new looks. The more you flex this styling muscle, the easier it will become. Promise.

If you are not able to create a look on your Outfit Planner because you weren't able to find items while shopping last week, go back to the Lookbooks (link below) and see if there is another outfit that works better with the current contents of your closet.

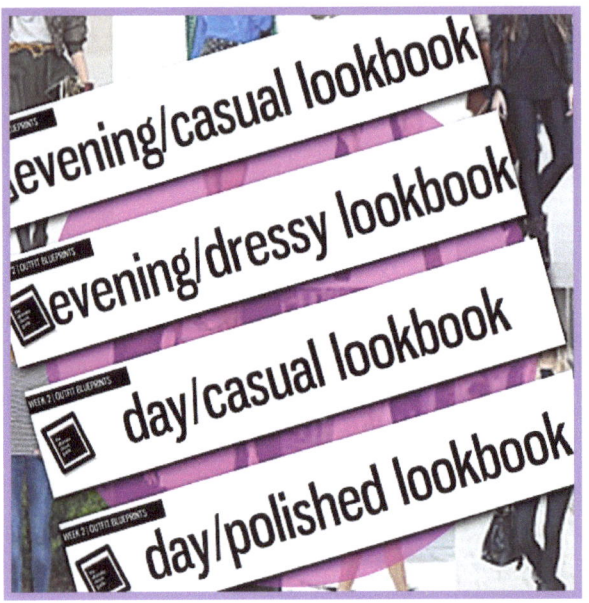

http://bit.ly/thelookbooks

- **BRITT'S TIP:** It's about inspiration not imitation remember? Sometimes you will need to improvise. These tools will help you do that so now is a great time to go with the fashion flow and get creative.

Go ahead and lay out your looks for the week using your printed look inspiration as you style-out what you have in your closet.

You don't have to stick to this exact schedule. You may wake up and feel like you want to wear Thursday's daytime look Tuesday afternoon. That is totally normal (let alone the story of my life), and you are prepared for that. It's about being flexible and removing the stress from the process of getting ready in the morning.

Life happens, weather happens, moods change, just know you can go with the flow. Nothing is written in stylist-stone.

Swap around outfits when you feel the need to do so. You want to update your look so you feel good walking out the door every day.

How To Lay Out Your Looks For The Week.

There are a few ways to get your outfits lined up for the week ahead in your closet. You could:

- Group all of the outfits together in one section of your closet (hanging-up with shoes/accessories on the floor underneath), and tape the appropriate printed inspiration look to the front hanger for each.

- Line your looks up on a dresser or the floor (now that you can actually see it) and place your Outfit Planner with printed looks nearby.

- Purchase a separate rolling rack (you can find inexpensive options on-line; this is also my method of choice when lining up looks) and move all of your upcoming outfits (accessories included) onto one rolling rack that sits outside of your closet.

Pick one method and go for it!

Now that your outfits are lined up for the week, you can get ready every day without having to think about it. It's a beautiful thing!

(week 3, step 2)

DAY 18: OUTFIT PLANNING FOR NEXT WEEK.

On or around Day 18, try to carve out thirty minutes to an hour of time. Screen shot of Week 3 below:

WEEK 3	DAY 15	DAY 16	DAY 17	DAY 18	DAY 19	DAY 20	DAY 21
	*Complete Week 3, Step 1	*Use Outfit Planner #1 *Follow-up on shopping list where needed	*Use Outfit Planner #1 *Follow-up on shopping list where needed	*Use Outfit Planner #1 *Steps 2 and 3	*Use Outfit Planner #1 *Follow-up on shopping list where needed	*Use Outfit Planner #1 *Follow-up on shopping list where needed	*Complete Week 3, Step 4 *Follow-up on shopping list where needed
	DAY 22	DAY 23	DAY 24	DAY 25	DAY 26	DAY 27	DAY 28

You will use this time to update your second Outfit Planner for next week. You can find the blank (you have already used the copy from the Closet Toolkit in this book) Outfit Planner template and download it on-line by following the link below: http://bit.ly/outfitplanners

Time to get a jumpstart on the week ahead! There is no need to go back to the drawing board and input all new looks for next week. It is an option, but it is not necessary, especially if you are limited on time.

Instead, take note of the looks that are working well this week and carry those over into next week.

Whatever you do decide to carry over, I am going to challenge you to change up in one, small way. This will flex that styling muscle of yours.

It could be anything from a change of shoe or bag, to changing up your lip color or hairstyle.

This will get you thinking and playing with your closet a bit, which is exactly where you want to be at this point in the process.

Above all, you want to have fun with this! If you get stuck, go back to your printed looks for inspiration.

(week 3, step 3)

DAY 18 CONTINUED: MID-WEEK SHOPPING LIST CHECK-UP.

If you're shopping on-line, today is your day to follow-up on anything else from your 80/20 Shopping List that you may not have found last week.

You don't need to shop every week. Go with what works for your life and budget, this step is just a suggestion.

For On-line Shoppers:

Order on-line today and tomorrow (Days 18 and 19 on your 30-Day Calendar, screen shot below) if you can, so you will have items delivered sooner than later.

	DAY 15	DAY 16	DAY 17	DAY 18	DAY 19	DAY 20	DAY 21
WEEK 3	*Complete Week 3, Step 1	*Use Outfit Planner #1 *Follow-up on shopping list where needed	*Use Outfit Planner #1 *Follow-up on shopping list where needed	*Use Outfit Planner #1 *Steps 2 and 3	*Use Outfit Planner #1 *Follow-up on shopping list where needed	*Use Outfit Planner #1 *Follow-up on shopping list where needed	*Complete Week 3, Step 4 *Follow-up on shopping list where needed
	DAY 22	DAY 23	DAY 24	DAY 25	DAY 26	DAY 27	DAY 28

You can try everything on and incorporate the items you keep into next week's Outfit Planner.

For In-store Shoppers:

Up for another round of shopping this weekend? Why not?

If it's in your budget and you have the time, today is the day to schedule a shopping date whether you're flying solo and/or partaking in some social shopping with friends.

(week 3, step 4)

DAY 21: OUTFIT PLANNER, ROUND 2.

At the end of Week 3 you'll have one Outfit Planner completed, and a new Planner in the works for next week. This is when you start to make the process your own.

Go back to your second Outfit Planner, and make any necessary changes for the week ahead. You may want to rework the Planner after you receive any new additions from your 80/20 shopping list this week.

Tomorrow, Day 22, is when you will pull your Week 4 Outfit Planner looks together. It's time to rinse and repeat!

{WEEK 4 + Bonus Days: Days 22 thru 30}

"It's time to start living the life you've imagined."

– Henry James

AFTER WEEK 4 YOU WILL:

Be in the Ultimate Closet zone, wearing way more than 20% of what is in your updated wardrobe, and mastering the entire shopping/styling process while you're at it.

THE WEEK 4 CLOSET TOOLKIT INCLUDES:

✗ Reference all tools from the Week 2 Closet Toolkit in the beginning of this guide

TO HAVE ON HAND:

✗ Your 30-Day Calendar

✗ Your 80/20 Shopping List

✗ Last Week's Outfit Planner & a new Outfit Planner worksheet

✗ tape

✗ scissors

✗ printer

Welcome to the home stretch, or rather, welcome to the beginning of your Ultimate Closet lifestyle.

You're in the fashion flow of it all. Let's bring it on home!

{WEEK 4, STEPS 1-4}

(week 4, step 1)

DAY 22: OUTFIT PLANNER, ROUND 2.

Check your 30-Day calendar and adjust it to line up with your schedule this week. You are in the driver's seat.

	DAY 22	DAY 23	DAY 24	DAY 25	DAY 26	DAY 27	DAY 28
WEEK 4	*Complete Week 4, Step 1	*Use Outfit Planner #2 *Follow-up on shopping list where needed	*Use Outfit Planner #2 *Follow-up on shopping list where needed	*Use Outfit Planner #2 *Complete Week 4, Steps 2 and 3	*Use Outfit Planner #2 *Follow-up on shopping list where needed	*Use Outfit Planner #2 *Follow-up on shopping list where needed	*Follow-up on shopping list where needed

I've selected Day 22 (usually a Sunday) to be the date you lay out your Outfit Planner looks for the week, but if that doesn't work, try to find a set time you will be able to commit thirty minutes to at the start each week.

Similar to last week, go ahead and line up your outfits for the week using whatever method works best for you. You now have a full week worth of outfits lined up for every occasion on your calendar, and the flexibility to change it up if you need/want to!

(week 4, step 2)

DAY 25: MID-WEEK OUTFIT PLANNING.

Similar to last week, this is your mid-week Outfit Planning time.

At this point you will have a week and a half of updated looks you have tried under your belt, along with a few new shopping options to add into the outfit mix.

	DAY 22	DAY 23	DAY 24	DAY 25	DAY 26	DAY 27	DAY 28
WEEK 4	*Complete Week 4, Step 1	*Use Outfit Planner #2 *Follow-up on shopping list where needed	*Use Outfit Planner #2 *Follow-up on shopping list where needed	*Use Outfit Planner #2 *Complete Week 4, Steps 2 and 3	*Use Outfit Planner #2 *Follow-up on shopping list where needed	*Use Outfit Planner #2 *Follow-up on shopping list where needed	*Follow-up on shopping list where needed

Now it's time to pick and chose the looks you want to move forward with next week (you can refresh looks from last week or head back to the Lookbooks for inspiration) and incorporate any new closet additions you may have received after shopping these past couple of weeks.

Follow this link to get to your Lookbooks for additional inspiration: http://bit.ly/thelookbooks

Follow this link to print out a new Outfit Planner worksheet: http://bit.ly/outfitplanners

As I mentioned last week, there is no need to try out all new looks every week. It's fun, but if it stresses you out, stick with what works and make small adjustments to refresh things a bit.

• **BRITT'S TIP:** The Outfit Blueprint is something you can really build a sense of updated, personal style with. Once you have a couple of go-to Outfit Blueprints (i.e. outfits) that work for daytime and evening occasions, you can use them as your fashion foundation for the rest of the season.

All you need to change things up is a simple style tweak here and there in the form of an accessory, added layer, etc. Less can be so much more!

Guess Who's Wearing More Than 20% Of What's In Their Closet? You Are.

As you start to input looks for your third Outfit Planner worksheet, it is time to pause and reflect because you are almost at the end of your 30-day ride…

Notice how you are working with fewer items in your closet (even though you have a select few new additions from the 80/20 Shopping List) and are creating more updated outfits than you probably have in the past six months. This is huge! Pat yourself on the back, and then move on to Step 3.

(week 4, step 3)

DAY 25 CONTINUED: SHOPPING LIST CHECK-UP.

Similar to last week (Week 3, Step 3), take a moment to see where you are in your shopping process.

Do you need to schedule additional shopping time to cover your high-priority 80/20 Shopping List items or are you all set?

If you are still plugging away, schedule your in-store shopping for the week and/or follow-up on any on-line items you need to get. I'll leave you to it because you're a pro now.

THE 30-DAY ULTIMATE CLOSET GUIDE

(week 4, step 4)

BONUS DAYS 29 & 30.

You made it!

If you are at all like me and hardly ever take the time to recognize your achievements, take these two bonus days and revel in what you have created.

Buy a cake, twirl around in your closet, document your gorgeous wardrobe with copious and heavily filtered (even though you don't need it) pictures on Instagram, or pop a bottle of bubbly and toast to your Ultimate Closet!

Whatever feels right to you, do it. Take a moment to celebrate and enjoy what you have created.

When you go into your Ultimate Closet this week, stop and soak up how amazing everything looks, all because you decided to take a little time for yourself and make big things happen! Well done.

SO, HOW FAR HAVE YOU COME IN 30 DAYS? HERE'S THE RECAP:

✗ You performed a complete Closet Overhaul and made space for amazing things to come in. Major.

✗ You learned how to focus in on updated looks that work for your life. Who needs a personal stylist anyway?

✗ You created a masterful seasonal Shopping List that will simplify your shopping process for rest of the year. You are a *shopping ninja* if I ever saw one.

✗ You have styled your own looks, updated your own wardrobe, organized and simplified your own life, and hello... you now have your ULTIMATE CLOSET!

Congratulations & cheers!

NEXT STEPS.

Keep going and keep mixing it up! See something and you're just not sure if it is for you? Try it on. Try it on. Oh, right, try it on. Got it?

Try to push yourself out of your personal style comfort zones at least once a month, if not once a week and bring your friends into the picture as often as you can. Sharing is caring.

I wish you a lifetime filled with feeling confident in what you're wearing as you walk out the door. That is what it is all about.

This may be the end of the 30-Day Ultimate Closet Guide, but really, it is just the beginning…

UPDATES.

There will be all kinds of updates going on over here. This entire guide along with the Closet Toolkits, will change a bit with each year and season. Stay in the loop and get access to the latest by subscribing to my mailing list here:

http://bit.ly/ultimateclosetguidesubscribe

I wish you all the best, from my Ultimate Closet, to yours.

did you like it?
share it with a friend!

see more at:
www.ultimateclosetguide.com

brought to you by,
the style shaker

CLOSET TOOLKIT LINKS:

WEEK 1

1. 30 DAY CALENDAR- http://bit.ly/30daycalendar
2. BABY PREP 2- http://bit.ly/besthangers
3. CLOSET CONTRACT- http://bit.ly/closetcontract
4. CLOSET INVITATION- http://bit.ly/closetinvitation
5. CLOSET ZEN & CHEAT SHEET (TEAR OUT FROM BOOK)
6. CLOSET ORG INSPIRATION LIST- http://bit.ly/closetinspiration
7. CLOSET TO CASH LIST- http://bit.ly/closettocash
8. SHARE YOUR WEEK 1 STORIES- http://bit.ly/tellyourclosetstory

WEEK 2

1. LOOKBOOK- http://bit.ly/thelookbooks
2. BODY TYPE GUIDE- http://bit.ly/bodytypeguide
3. 80/20 SHOPPING LIST- http://bit.ly/8020shoppinglist
4. CORE SHOPPING LIST- http://bit.ly/coreitems
5. TREND SHOPPING LIST- http://bit.ly/trenditems
6. ON-LINE SHOPPING HIT LIST- http://bit.ly/shoppinghitlist
7. STYLESHAKER SHOPPING LIST- http://bit.ly/styleshakershoppinglist

CLOSET TOOLKIT LINKS:

WEEKS 3 & 4

1. LOOKBOOK- http://bit.ly/thelookbooks
2. OUTFIT PLANNER TEMPLATE- http://bit.ly/outfitplanners
3. SUBSCRIBE- http://bit.ly/ultimateclosetguidesubscribe

THE 30-DAY ULTIMATE CLOSET GUIDE

See more on:

the style shaker

www.thestyleshaker.com

ACKNOWLEDGEMENTS

If you're at all like me, you get to this section in a book, glance briefly, and turn the page without a second thought.

Instead of going the (long-winded) traditional route, I'd like to use this space to say:

"Thank you for being a part of The 30-Day Ultimate Closet Guide."

I wrote this book with one goal in mind, to inspire you.
I hope I have succeeded.

BRITTANY WITKIN

MORE ULTIMATE CLOSET LOVE...

"Now when I flip through fashion magazines I think, 'Hmmm, I could do that!' In the past, I'd flip, flip, flip and think, 'there's no way I could pull that trend off.' My eyes have been opened and my style is evolving every day." -Ami Doshi, Director of Global Outreach/Mother

"I no longer dread getting ready. The thinking is already done for me! I just pick a look and go. I know I'll look put together every time. This guide is such a life saver!" -Sara Tallent, Entrepreneur/Photographer/Mother

BRITTANY WITKIN is a style expert that has revolutionized the wardrobes & closets of hundreds of clients across the country whether it's in-person, on-line, or via her *30-Day Ultimate Closet Guide* (digital and paperback) so every woman, everywhere is empowered to create the wardrobe she has always wanted.

Before launching her own styling business TheStyleShaker.com, Witkin spent over a decade at luxury retail institution Neiman Marcus where she fine-tuned her fashion skills curating assortments for multi-million dollar purchase orders in the buying office and leading the creative direction behind e-commerce projects on both NeimanMarcus.com & LastCall.com.

Since leaving the corporate landscape, Witkin has been featured by fashion media outlets across the country and continues to speak at fashion events and workshops spreading her empowering message and enabling other women to create the closet and life they've always wanted.

You can follow her latest styling projects and more at www.thestyleshaker.com.

www.ingramcontent.com/pod-product-compliance
Lightning Source LLC
Chambersburg PA
CBHW042325150426
43192CB00004B/117